MULTISENSORY
God Connections

Actively Growing Closer to God

Linda Van Soest Tintle

ISBN 979-8-88644-272-4 (Paperback)
ISBN 979-8-88644-273-1 (Digital)

Covenant Books
11661 Hwy 707
Murrells Inlet, SC 29576
www.covenantbooks.com

CHAPTER 1

A Spiritual Growth Quest

I'd like to explain how writing this book came about. It evolved from the following:

- A desire

    Several years ago, I had a growing desire for a closer connection with God, as my relationship with God was being crowded out by all my responsibilities. I started to think of ways I could focus on some spiritual qualities throughout my days of teaching, being a wife and a mom of four children, as I also increasingly became more involved in the care of my aging father. My sporadic morning and bedtime devotions were not enough to provide the relationship I wanted.

- Being too busy

    My busyness led me to brainstorm ways I could make time for God within my daily routine. How could I feel His presence, guidance, and help throughout the day—not just in my morning and evening prayers? Even when I did have the time—or I should say, when I *took* the time—to have devotions, I found that later that same day, I often couldn't even remember what I had read about.

- A specific focus

> One Sunday in church, while reciting the "first and great commandment"—"Love the Lord thy God with all thy heart, with all thy soul, with all thy mind, and with all thy strength…" (Luke 10:27)—as we do every Sunday during worship, the question popped into my mind: "Am I doing that? Am I loving the Lord with all my heart, soul, mind, and strength? What does that actually mean, anyway?"

At first glance, it seems so obvious—we are to love God first and foremost and with all of our being. Yet *how* can loving God so completely be carried out in daily everyday life? It occurred to me that while I had heard several sermons and/or read books or devotionals on the second part of this verse, "Love thy neighbor as thyself," I didn't remember sermons on what it means in a practical sense to actually love God with all my heart, with all my soul, with all my mind, and with all my strength. This verse became the focus and title of my spiritual meditations and efforts to grow spiritually.

In trying to fully understand how to love God with all my heart, soul, mind, and strength and how to obey *this first and greatest commandment*, I began to look up the location of this verse in the Bible. I was amazed to find that *this command can be found in eight different places*, including books in both the Old Testament and the New Testament: Deuteronomy 6: 4–7, Deuteronomy 26:16, Jeremiah 24:7, Jeremiah 31:33, 1 Samuel 7:3, Matthew 22:37–39, Mark 12:28–31, and Luke 10:27.

This fact just reinforces to me the great importance and significance of this verse and solidifies my determination to work at understanding it and trying to carry it out.

- A commitment

In pursuit of understanding this command, I asked myself, "What do I love with all my heart, soul, mind, and strength?" I took note of and analyzed what most of my thoughts, my innermost desires, and my passions were related to. I discovered that *my family* and *what I wanted myself and my family to do and to accomplish far outweighed the number of thoughts and desires for a close connection with God.* This showed me what I truly valued. While those aren't necessarily wrong desires, we are *commanded* to put God above all else, including family. I made a sincere commitment to try to love God with all my heart, soul, mind, and strength in practical ways in my everyday life.

- Faith

I believed that I would be able to grow spiritually and to have a closer connection with God if I prayed about it, if I took the time to be still to sense God's presence, and if I took the time to work at it. I found it to be very important to truly *believe* that since this goal is something in line with God's will, He would bring it to pass. I have experienced peace and joy after purposely affirming my faith in being able to gain deeper closeness to God with His help.

- Study and research

With this verse as the focus of my spiritual growth, I devoted a spiritual or devotional journal to the topic, "Love the Lord your God with all your heart, with all your soul, with all your mind, and with all your strength."

I started to do research about the meaning of loving God and the biblical meanings of *heart, soul, mind,* and *strength.* I started to write down my findings, my thoughts, my questions, and my insights. I began to collect related scripture verses, as well as quotes from other sources that were related to understanding this verse.

- A learning process

When I first decided to work on understanding what this verse means, I thought of it as a short-term topic or theme that I would focus on for a while. Years later, as I am still working on trying to put this command into practice, I realize that this aim to love God with all my heart, soul, mind, and strength is a *lifelong process*. I am not going to reach a point where I "totally get it" and am able to totally carry it out. This study has become an attempt to *learn to love God* completely. While I will never fully reach the end goal while here on earth, I aim to make progress and to keep moving in the right direction. The title of my project now became "Learning to love the Lord your God with all your heart, with all your mind, with all your soul, and with all your strength."

An "aha" moment occurred to me one day. I realized that I was utilizing *evidence-based and proven learning strategies* that I used for years as a teacher of children and young adults. Now as a learner and student of spiritual content, I became aware that I had not used these engaging methods before in my personal devotional times or during other attempts to learn spiritually. I was now experiencing first-hand what it meant to be *engaged in my spiritual learning*. I found that these research-based techniques for enhancing learning in other content areas in academic educational settings could also be used effectively in learning to love the Lord. I am excited to apply these learning strategies and methods to my spiritual learning attempts.

- Learning strategies

    The most effective way to learn anything is to be *fully engaged and active* in the learning process. As I began to look up definitions, refer to scriptural commentaries, memorize related verses, and write my thoughts and insights to work at understanding this verse, I realized that I was becoming *engaged* in my attempt to learn. When I took the time to copy, write down, and memorize certain verses, *I became more actively engaged and I began to learn.*

- Active and engaged learning

    Looking up the definition of *engage* gave some added insight (boldface added).

    - "occupy, attract or **involve (someone's interest or attention)**" (Google Dictionary)
    - **"to attract and hold fast"** (Dictionary.com)
    - **"to interest someone in something and keep them thinking about it"** (Cambridge Dictionary)
    - **"to make someone feel excited, enthusiastic, or impressed"** (Macmillan Dictionary)
    - **"If you engage with someone or a group of people, you get involved with that thing or group and feel that you are connected with it or have real contact with it"** (Collinsdictionary.com [intransitive verb definition])

    Synonyms of *engage* are **(to) captivate, (to) fascinate, (to) enchant**" (Collins Dictionary); **"(to) absorb, engross, immerse"** (Merriam-Webster.com). It can be concluded that "engaged learning" **means being actively involved in the learning process.**

- Personal reflection

  Applying the definitions and synonyms for *engage* to the methods I used for spiritual growth showed me clearly that my spiritual learning was not *engaging*. I wasn't enthusiastic, totally or actively involved in, connected with, fascinated or engrossed in my spiritual learning. *Active and engaged learning requires involvement, participation, and work* compared to passive learning or spoon-fed learning. Based on this realization, I once again revised the title of my project and spiritual focus. It is now "Actively learning to love the Lord your God with all your heart, with all your soul, with all your mind, and with all your strength."

- Organizing my findings

  I began to do some research and study what is meant in the Bible by *heart*, by *soul*, by *mind*, and by *strength*. I wrote down insights I read in a Bible concordance, in Bible commentaries, and in other sources. I was accumulating quite a bit of information, which I began to organize. As I grouped together similar insights, my understanding grew. Also, I found I could remember my insights more easily. This journaling process was another engaging learning method that enhanced my learning.

- Chapter organization

  The remaining chapters of this book (except for the last chapter) are focused on the parts of this verse in sequential order. This technique is similar to a teaching method Rick Warren uses, which is called…

  [T]he "pronounce it" method of biblical meditation. You start with a verse and read it over and over again. Each time you read the verse, you emphasize a different word. It's the simplest way to start unlocking scripture. ("Bible Study: Focus on One Word at a Time" by Rick Warren, idisciple.org)

Chapter 2: Actively Learning
Chapter 3: To Love the Lord Your God
Chapter 4: With All Your Heart
Chapter 5: With All Your Soul
Chapter 6: With All Your Mind
Chapter 7: With All Your Strength
Chapter 8: Conclusion

In these subsequent chapters, I share ideas and strategies that help me become engaged in and actively involved in learning how to love God in my everyday life.

CHAPTER 2

Actively Learning

("to love the Lord your God with all your heart, with all your soul, with all your mind, and with all your strength")

In this chapter and the next five chapters, I begin by looking into the secular meanings of the words of my spiritual growth focus and then move to considering the biblical meanings of those words.

A Secular Perspective on "Actively Learning"

As mentioned in the previous chapter, the qualities of engagement and active involvement are crucial to all meaningful learning, including spiritual learning. Secular meanings of the words *actively* and *learning* can add to the understanding of being an active spiritual learner.

Online definitions of *actively* include (boldface added):

- **"in a deliberate** and **positive way; in a vigorous way"** (Google Dictionary)
- **"characterized by energetic work, participation; involving physical effort and action"** (Dictionary.com)
- **"with the aim of making something happen** rather than just hoping that it will; **in a practical way"** (Macmillan Dictionary)

Definitions of *learning* include (boldface added):

- "**knowledge acquired by systemic study** in any field of scholarly application" (Dictionary.com)
- "**modification of a behavioral tendency**' (Merriam-Webster.com) (modification of habits)

I can form a definition of "active learning" based on this secular definition:

> Knowledge that is acquired through systematic study and through modification of a behavioral tendency in a way that is deliberate and positive, that is vigorous, characterized by energetic work and participation, involving physical effort, with the aim of making something happen in a practical way.

This definition of learning is also relevant (Boldface added):

> Learning involves **strengthening correct responses** and **weakening incorrect responses.** Learning involves **adding new information to your memory**. Learning involves making sense of the presented material by **attending to relevant information, mentally reorganizing it, and connecting it with what you already know**." (#8 of 10 definitions of learning by Connie Malamed, from "Learning and the Science of Instruction" by Ruth C. Clark and Richard E. Mayer)

Many of the strategies that I have used to grow spiritually are related to the components of this last definition:

- *strengthening* effective responses and *habits*;

- *getting rid of ineffective responses*;
- working at building up and *adding to my memory*;
- reorganizing my thoughts to *make associations and connections* throughout my day.

Educational Research on Effective Learning

The results of research in the field of learning show that "engaging students in the learning process *increases their attention and focus*, motivates them to practice higher-level critical thinking skills, and promotes meaningful learning experiences" (teaching.washington.edu>engaging students in learning). *The most effective way to learn anything is to be fully engaged or actively involved in the process* as opposed to attempting to learn in ways that are passive.

We are more fully engaged when we use two or more of our senses. If we read silently, we are using one sense: our vision. When we read out loud, we become more engaged because we are employing our voices, as well as our hearing (as we hear our own voice), together with our vision. In teaching, this is called using a multisensory approach, which for years has been a widely used research-based method for teaching special education students. In recent years, multisensory methods have also become widely used in regular education classrooms because of their *proven effectiveness for all learners*.

> The benefits of multisensory learning have been verified by contemporary research in cognitive science… We remember how to do things best when the directions we're given engage multiple senses… As long as the activity engages multiple areas of the brain, it can help students develop stronger memories…(Waterford.org>why multisensory learning is an effective strategy for teaching)

Different Types of Intelligences

Harvard psychologist Howard Gardner has proposed that there are multiple kinds of intelligences. He theorizes that "people do not have just an intellectual capacity, but have many kinds of intelligence, including musical, interpersonal, intrapersonal, spatial-visual, linguistic, logical-mathematical, bodily-kinesthetic and naturalistic intelligences… Many teachers utilize multiple intelligences in their teaching philosophies and work to integrate Gardner's theory into the classroom" (verywellmind.com).

Acting upon this theory means providing learning activities, as well as ways to express one's learning, that cater to different intelligences. I feel that this theory can and should be applied to spiritual growth as well as to academic learning. Meaningful learning takes place when a person's unique individual intelligences and learning preferences are taken into consideration. I have included some ideas for addressing multiple intelligences in each chapter.

Scriptural Foundations

The Bible supports the idea of *being active* in our love and faith. Some verses relating to "act" and "taking action" are (boldface added):

But **prove yourselves doers of the word, and not merely hearers**…(James 1: 22 ESV)

Let us not love in word or talk but in deed and in truth. (1 John 3:18 ESV)

So whoever knows the right thing to do and fails to do it, for him **it is sin**. (James 4:17 ESV)

Therefore, **preparing your minds for action**…(1 Peter 1:13 ESV)

> The **people who know their God shall
> stand firm and take action.** (Daniel 11:32, ESV)

The topic of *learning* is also addressed in the Bible. Some verses relating to wisdom, knowledge, and learning include (boldface added):

> For this very reason, **make every effort to
> supplement** your faith with virtue, and **virtue
> with knowledge.** (2 Peter 1:5 ESV)

> **But grow in grace and knowledge of our
> Lord** and Savior Jesus Christ. (2 Peter 3:18)

> Take my yoke upon you and **learn from
> me**, for I am gentle and humble in heart, and you
> will find rest for your souls. (Matthew 11:29)

> **Keep this Book of the Law always on
> your lips; meditate on it day and night,** so that
> you may be careful to do everything written in it.
> (Joshua 1:8)

As Christians and disciples of Christ, we need to be constantly learning. This quote from a devotional booklet written by my dad addresses this: "A disciple is one who remains teachable. The Christian is always a pupil of Jesus Christ. He/she is a student" (B. Van Soest, Disciple booklet).

There are numerous biblical references to the importance of becoming childlike in our relationship to God so that we become trusting and humble, moldable and transformable, and open-minded to God's will. Those same qualities apply to being a teachable student. I accept the fact that my spiritual life is not what it should be and that I cannot truly and perfectly "love God with all my heart, with all my soul, with all my mind, and with all my strength." But I want to be in the process of growing and learning to love God the way He intends. I need to have the mindset of "progress, not perfection" (a famous quote from Alcoholics Anonymous). This quote from Jenny Allen's book, *Restless*, spoke to me and motivated me to make changes in my daily life: "I think in twenty years we will regret more of the things we didn't do than things we did imperfectly" (p. 53).

I don't want to have regrets about not taking the time to learn and grow in my spiritual life. These quotes from biblereasons.com are also instructive and powerful:

> **Learning is a blessing from the Lord. Are you growing in your knowledge of God and His work? The wisdom from the Bible prepares, cautions, encourages, comforts, guides and supports us in our time of need.**
>
> **Develop a passion for learning. If you do, you will never cease to grow.**
>
> **The capacity to learn is a gift; the ability to learn is a skill; the willingness to learn is a choice.**
>
> **As you age you should be progressing in life. You should be growing and maturing. Your relationship with Christ should be deepening as well. As you spend time with Christ and get to know more of who He is, then your intimacy with Him will increase. You will then begin to experience Him more throughout your week.**

I am choosing to be a spiritual student: to study, to learn, and to work on gaining a deeper understanding of what it means to love God.

Spiritual Insights

At a time when my life was especially busy and stressful, I was continually evaluating my priorities and searching for the peace that

I was making the right choices. I needed to feel God's presence and help throughout my busy days, and I had a strong desire to grow spiritually.

Reading the above quote about always being a pupil of Christ caused me to evaluate how seriously I took my spiritual growth. Did my actions of going to church, perhaps reading a daily devotional, and participating in an occasional Bible study group really show commitment to being a Christian student? For me, those practices alone didn't provide *daily* engagement in my spiritual learning or *daily* spiritual connectedness or *daily* opportunities for growth. I began to pursue what it means to be *committed daily* to actively learn and grow as a Christian.

After gathering the secular and biblical definitions of *active* and *learning*, I also asked myself: "Am I working at my spiritual growth in a deliberate and energetic way and preparing my mind for action? Am I making every effort to supplement my faith with knowledge? Am I excited and enthusiastic about my time with God, my devotional time, and my spiritual learning?"

An honest assessment indicated to me that *I had not been engaged in or actively involved in my spiritual learning. In the past, I had been a passive spiritual learner.* My learning methods were basically just reading, listening to sermons, and praying silently. Most of the time, I did not find it captivating or fascinating, and I really wasn't putting much effort or energy into it. My mind often wandered to other things. I rarely felt a deep spiritual connectedness and I didn't have much long-term learning from my devotions. By mid-morning, the main points of what I had read earlier that morning were often forgotten.

Conclusion

I came to the conclusion that in order for effective spiritual learning to take place,

- I need to have the *desire to learn spiritually* followed by *commitments* to make time for it, work at it, and to make it a priority. *(And, really, what is more important or a higher priority more lasting, more relevant, and a better investment of my time than my* relationship *with* God? *Nothing else really matters.)*

- I need to *make a deliberate, positive decision* to learn and grow spiritually.
- I need to *energetically and enthusiastically take action* upon the goal of having a daily spiritual connection.
- I need to *choose to make something happen* (with prayer and with God's help).
- I need to *work on learning in a practical way.*
- I need to *act daily* if I want to actively learn to love the Lord.
- I need to *commit now, today*—not at some point in the future—to having a growing relationship and connection with God. I need to "just do it," as Nike says. (What's holding me back?)
- I need to *continually recommit* to this goal, as I can easily get caught up in the goings-on of the day.

Educational Principles

Making a commitment to be a "spiritual student" and realizing my passive learning habits for spiritual growth, I started to use more multisensory methods in my devotional and prayer times.

After using these techniques for some time, I experienced the effectiveness of being engaged in my spiritual learning. Being more actively involved has brought me insights and a deeper connection with God. Using multisensory methods is one change that enhanced my spiritual growth.

Below are some of the techniques I use daily in order to be a more active learner:

- *reading and praying out loud.* In Joyce Meyer's book, *The Secret Power of Speaking God's Word,* she explains her experience:

  > In 1976 God graciously granted me revelation on the power of confessing His Word out loud… I began confessing God's Word out loud twice a day. I can honestly say **that was the beginning of wonderful changes in me**… **I strongly encourage you to confess the Word of God out loud daily.** (pgs. ix, x, and xvi of the Introduction, boldface added)

- *copying down verses that have personal meaning*
- *reflecting, writing down insights as well as questions*
- *doing some "soul-searching" and drawing conclusions*
- *deciding on proactive measures*
- *doing research*
- *incorporating movement and motions to singing hymns and praise songs*

Strategies to Work on Loving God More Fully

From the onset of this "spiritual quest," my desire has been to discover practical ways to learn to love God more fully. How can I take time to connect with God during a full and busy day? While I truly want to put God first, life for me, as for most of us, continues to hold a myriad of demands and responsibilities. I have incorporated *doable* and *practical ways to connect with God more often during the day* while continuing to live a busy life.

Acknowledging that learning doesn't happen overnight was important for me. A lot of time and patience were necessary to form new habits and routines. Over a period of time, I have *formed new habits that allow for learning to love God more completely through a more constant relationship with Him.*

It was also helpful to realize that learning usually occurs in small parts, in a step-by-step, insight-by-insight fashion. I found this quote by van Gogh to be very encouraging: **"Great things are done by a series of small things brought together."**

I made *a series of small changes in my routines*, making changes in some of my habits and forming some new habits. I started to think of ways to remember God's presence throughout the day. I feel I am building up a *great thing* in my spiritual life through these small everyday changes.

An Acronym to Remember Spiritual Connection Strategies

As I found and utilized more ways that helped me spiritually, I formed an acronym with the first letters of the strategies that I used. Ironically and appropriately, the acronym is ACT2 (ACT squared). There are two words for each of the letters of the acronym.

A-ssociations made between specific daily routines and a specific way to connect to God

A-wareness of God's presence in my surroundings as I perform daily tasks

C-hanging some of my daily routines to make time for spiritual growth

C-hoosing different habits and practices, realizing I can choose to try to love God more completely

T-hroughout the day and throughout all I do, trying to mentally connect with God

T-otal engagement in spiritual learning and connectedness

Specific ways I have incorporated each of the actions of this acronym into my day are:

Associations

Over time, I have made *specific* associations *between some of my daily routines and a thought or action that connects me to God*. Creating an *association* between a particular routine activity and a specific mental spiritual act—such as an act of praise, prayer, or scripture recitation—has been very powerful and very helpful for me. By purposely associating certain songs, hymns, verses, or prayers with various routines that I do daily, I have been *able to easily add frequent times of spiritual connectedness to a regular day*. I particularly like this quote: "Even the most routine part of your day can be a spiritual act of worship, holy and pleasing to Me (God)" (*Jesus Calling*, Sarah Young, p. 269).

Another quote that speaks strongly to me is, "In a word, **to let the spirit... Grow up through the common**" (William Ellery Channing from "My Symphony" in Friends of Silence, Vol. XXXIII, No. 8, boldface added).

Some of my routine associations are:

- During my *morning shower*, I sing a praise song three or four times. In the past, my morning would start with my mind racing with an agenda for the day, focused on what I needed to do or could choose to do. I have replaced those thoughts with praising God, thanking Him and trying to place a priority on connecting with Him. This association has become so strong that now when I get in the shower, I automatically begin singing to praise and thank God. This refocusing strategy is a reminder that it's not all about me, my plans, and my projects. This practice of singing a praise song first thing in the morning is a way that I aim to "let my world not be centered on me but on Thee" (John Baillie, *A Diary of Private Prayer*).

- My *morning exercises and stretches* have become associated with a time to connect spiritually. While doing my exercises, I sing either out loud or to myself in my head specific hymns or praise songs that are associated with the movements. My exercises have become a worshipful experience for me, through which I acknowledge God's greatness and my weakness, as I lift up my thoughts to Him, aiming to be open to His leading.
- *Hair and makeup routine*—I have memorized 1 Peter 3:3–4 (NIV): "Your beauty should not come from outward adornment...rather, it should be that of your inner self, the unfading beauty of a gentle and quiet spirit, which is of great worth in God's sight." I say this verse to myself to remember to focus on having inner beauty and a quiet and gentle spirit.
- *Going for a walk/walking the dog* has become a time to be observant of nature and to connect to Him through His creation, acknowledging His power and control over all. I have also made the purposeful association of praying for others while I walk. This is a way I am working on balance in my prayers and a way to daily address the names and issues on my prayer list.
- *The practice of putting in prescribed eyedrops* two times a day is now associated with singing a chosen praise song in my head. This practice encourages me to keep my head tilted back for the duration of the song and is another opportunity to focus on God for a few minutes rather than be absorbed with my to-do list.
- *The scent of a candle* and/or the flame of a candle has now become associated with the "infusion" of God's spirit everywhere, His *mystery*, and the awe and wonder of His incomprehensible spirit.

Awareness

I know that God is omnipresent and that He is with me every-where at all times. It is my aim to have a constant awareness of this fact. *I can more often tap into an awareness of God's presence by*

- *taking a few minutes to be still* several times during the day, focusing on that fact that God is everywhere, that He is with me;
- being *more attuned to nature*—the weather, the sky, the wind—trying to be aware through all my senses, truly see-ing and sensing nature instead of taking it for granted;
- *bringing into the house items of nature* (such as flowers, leafy branches, etc.) These serve as visual reminders to ponder the amazing detail, pattern, and design in all of creation. I've trained my brain to associate God's power and presence when I see and pass by those items of nature in the house;
- *memorizing Bible verses that refer to various parts of nature*, associating a specific verse with a specific part of creation as a way to redirect my thoughts to the Creator and sense Him through nature.

Changes

Making changes *in my daily routine—basically, forming new hab-its—has helped me be more connected to God.* I found that I needed to commit to using a specific learning strategy or means of engagement *every day for three weeks*—the amount of time research shows that it takes for something to become a habit—in order to feel its benefits. By forming new habits that provide ways of connecting with God during daily routines, I have experienced a deeper sense of peace, more frequent joy, and overwhelming sense of gratitude.

Changes I've made are:

- *Writing in a gratitude journal daily (or almost every day).* Taking the time to actually write down ten things I am grateful for every day puts an emphasis on all that I have instead of getting caught up in feelings of discontent or wishing for different circumstances.

- *Multiple daily prayers of thanks and gratitude.* I used to think I was a thankful person. When I analyzed what most of my prayers were about, I found I was *asking* more than *thanking*. I now try to stop numerous times during each day just to express my thanks and gratitude to God.
- *Memorization of hymn and praise song lyrics.* Several years ago, I decided to memorize all four stanzas of a hymn that focuses on God's holiness in an attempt to raise my thoughts to God, particularly when I felt weighed down by challenges and difficulties. I found that singing this hymn, either out loud or just in my head, was great for what I call TRT (Thought Replacement Therapy). Memorizing a hymn or praise song allows me to change my thoughts at any time in any place. I have now memorized several hymns and praise songs that I sing every day. This strategy has been an effective way to "retrain my brain."
- *Stopping to be* still. This has been a difficult change for me, but I have found that it helps me to get in touch with myself and my feelings, to relax, and to reconnect with God. The instruction in the verse, "Be still and know that I am God" (Psalm 46:10) has been crucial for me.

Choices

I aim to *make spiritually right choices.* Various choices are available in numerous small and big decisions throughout my day.

- The *music I listen to.* Praise songs on Christian radio can redirect and lift up my mind, improving my attitude.
- Choosing to be *aware of my thoughts* and *making a choice to let go of negative thoughts*, replacing them with positive thoughts. Beverly Buncher, in the BALM program, makes the analogy of thoughts being like clouds that drift through

the sky. We can either focus on them or just let them drift on by.

- *How I spend my time*, realizing that stopping and being still for a period of time is often the best choice.
- Every morning, choosing *whether or not to take the time to write down ten things I am thankful for.*
- Every morning, making the choice as to *whether or not I do my exercises routine*, which has become a time to praise and worship and connect with God.
- Every morning, deciding *whether or not I will read a passage of the Bible or a devotional* and *whether or not I will be actively engaged in that devotional time*, prepared with paper and pen to be ready to "hear" and to grow.

Throughout

I think that part of the meaning of the command to "love God with all your heart, with all your soul, with all your mind, and with all your strength" directs us to love God throughout the whole day, every day as opposed to having isolated or compartmentalized times of worship and connectedness with Him just on Sundays or just during morning or evening devotional times. My goal has been to create habits and routines in which I connect with God *throughout* the day, not just in the morning or evening or in isolated devotional times.

Below are some ways I try to connect to God throughout the day.

- *Praying* throughout *the day.* I remember the Old Testament verse that instructed the Israelites to pray seven times a day. I now have a plan for aiming to pray at least seven times a day: first thing upon waking, at breakfast, in midmorning; at lunchtime, in midafternoon, at dinner, and at bedtime. I am working on strengthening this practice so that it becomes a habit. While I don't always say a verbal prayer before each meal, I am trying to remember to *pause* and *give thanks for the abundance of good food* that we have.

- *Praying* my way through *the day*, asking God for help and guidance *each hour* throughout the day. It's very easy to get absorbed in what I'm doing and get off track, so as every new hour starts, I try to reconnect and also take a minute to give Him thanks for His help during the previous hour. I find that it's not that difficult to do this, as I am usually aware of the time and when it is a new hour.

- I also am trying to remember to connect with God and sense His presence *throughout all I do*, remembering the verse, "Whatever you do, work at it with all you heart, as working for the Lord…" (Colossians 3:23 NIV).

Total

There is an ESL (English as a Second Language) technique called TPR, which stands for Total Physical Response. In this strategy, the teacher states a demonstrable action phrase in the new language while s/he modeling that action (i.e., s/he could say "I am putting on my coat" while actually putting on his/her coat). Then the students are asked to repeat the phrase out loud with the teacher while actually putting on their coats. This method has been proven to instill faster, longer-lasting, and more meaningful learning. I can apply a similar idea in my spiritual connection practices by using my total body or as many learning modalities as possible.

- *I use a TPR method while doing my physical exercises* that are associated with specific praise songs and hymns. Some examples are while singing the song, "Lord, I lift your name on high…" I actively step and move and lift up my arms and hands while singing the hymn, "Open my eyes that I may see…" I make wide arm circles to demonstrate opening up.

- I can *use a TPR* method when I aim to *let go* of cares and anxiety, to *surrender my will to God*, and *to lift up others in intercessory prayer* by physically acting out these desires with my hands and arms.

- *I recite verses about strength while doing strengthening exercises.*
- *I recite verses about walking in God's way while walking.*
- I can actually *bow down and kneel* while saying verses such as, "Come let us worship and bow down, let us kneel before the Lord our Maker" (Psalm 95:6), and *when giving prayers of gratitude.*
- I can *engage my total mind* by *reading scripture, a prayer, or devotional aloud with expression and passion,* followed by *writing down* thoughts or questions related to that reading.

Other Learning Theories to Apply to Spiritual Learning

- A key factor in effective learning in an educational setting is that a learner be *motivated to learn.* I have found the same to be true for my spiritual learning and growth—I need to truly want to learn, to be motivated to learn. If I just read a devotional or scripture passage as filling an obligation or something I feel I should do with no desire to learn or gain from it, it is all for naught.
- *Viewing each day as a fresh start* is a helpful attitude to have toward learning. Each day is a fresh new start to learning. Each new day also requires a fresh commitment or recommitment to learning. I need to make a commitment every day to learning what it means to love the Lord my God. It is so easy for me to slip into a routine centered on other things. It is a daily challenge for me to not let other things crowd out a connection with God.
- With my special education students, who have experienced much frustration and maybe failure in learning, I tried to instill confidence in their ability to learn. I used an approach called "can do," building and expanding upon what students already *can do* while building their confidence. I think this approach is true for all students, athletes, etc. The effectiveness of a coach who encourages his/

her athletes by telling them they *can do it* is an effective and good strategy. I've found this positive outlook to also be very true for my personal spiritual learning. I need to have the confidence, the belief, and the *faith* that I *can* learn and grow spiritually *with God's help*.

Additional Research-Based Effective Learning Strategies

Besides using multisensory methods to be more engaged and involved in my spiritual growth, there are other learning theories that I've used. I've listed these below, along with the ways I have applied them to my own spiritual learning.

- *Repetition, reviewing, rereading, and returning to are all important ways* to ensure learning, to help with memorization, and to bring about the internalization of material. We all know how something becomes ingrained in our brains after numerous exposures.

  I often reread all or part of the previous day's devotional. I also have found that by reading the same prayer book repeatedly over several years (the well-known classic, *A Diary of Private Prayer*, by theologian Dr. John Baillie), many of the prayers are now ingrained in my mind. My prayers have been truly molded and shaped because I have read his timeless prayers so many times. Almost always my prayers are in my own words, but often some of his eloquent and powerful prayer phrases come into my mind because I have read them so often.

- Exposure to the material in *various settings and various times of day*. When trying to memorize a verse or song lyrics, I have written the words down on cards and placed those cards in various rooms and places so that I see them frequently in different settings and during different times of the day.

- *Chunking* material into smaller, manageable parts as opposed to larger amounts of material. When trying to memorize the biblical qualities of love, the fruits and the gifts of the Holy Spirit, or the things scripture tells us our minds should be focused on, I have worked on memorizing a few at a time, adding more gradually until all are memorized.

- *Creative expression* of material gives us ownership of it and provides an in-depth learning experience that we can't plan or expect.

  I have employed numerous creative expression techniques in my spiritual quest, including writing poems, prayers, and my own lyrics to hymns and praise songs; using the Da Vinci method of "streamwriting" and/or stream-of-consciousness writing; doodling, painting, and concept drawing while meditating on a spiritual theme; journaling; and putting movements and motions to prayers, songs, and Bible verses.

- *Teaching and discussing with others.* This is a very strong method to learn something. Research backs this up ("Learning by teaching others is extremely effective..." BPS Research Digest, digest.bps.org.uk).

  Sharing my ideas with others by teaching them in a small group retreat, as well as in conversations, or writing down my ideas for others has been extremely helpful in clarifying and defining my ideas.

- *Meditating, reflecting, analyzing, and expanding upon* material. This is another way to deeply learn content, use higher-level critical thinking skills, and make associations and connections with other subject or content areas.

  During my times of being still or while lying awake in bed or while walking or exercising, it has been very helpful to meditate and reflect upon my reading and thoughts. Usually that is when my best insights have occurred.

- *Referring to the experts, doing research.* Biblical commentaries, Christian books, devotionals, the internet, etc. have all proven to be very helpful in order to gain understanding and insight.

- *Memorizing.* The Bible clearly states that we are to memorize scripture ("Let the word of Christ richly dwell within you" [Colossians 3:16]; "If you abide in Me, and My words abide in you…" [John 15:7]; "This book of law shall not depart from your mouth, but you shall meditate on it day and night" [Joshua 1:8]), yet this practice seems to be mainly forgotten today. In one article I read, the author states, "Half of us don't memorize scripture. Many of us have not even memorized a new verse in the last year" (ssnet.org). In recent years, I have found it very useful to have built up a "bank account" of verses in my memory from which I can make daily "withdrawals" to find words of comfort, wisdom, or guidance throughout the day. I definitely know that memorizing scripture is a way that I can love the Lord!

- *Using mnemonic devices* to remember key points, etc. I know the number of characteristics of love mentioned in 1 Corinthians 13, so when I want to focus on the qualities of biblical love, I know I need to think of sixteen characteristics; I know that there are nine fruits of the spirit, seven gifts of the spirit, and that there are eight things we are told to think on or think about. This method of counting the listed qualities in a verse has helped me remember those important biblical truths. The mnemonic devices of using acronyms or acrostics, singing Bible verses to a familiar hymn tune, or using other memory aids have all been advantageous to my scriptural knowledge.

- *Wordplay.* I often used alliteration to help me remember three or more points or concepts. For example, when I first started this spiritual quest, in order to remember what I wanted to work on, I focused on three words beginning with *P*—prayer, praise, patience. I later switched out the concepts to words beginning with the letter *L*—"lifting up my thoughts, looking to Jesus, loving others." The use of acronyms and acrostics mentioned above is also a form of wordplay that I use when I have an insight or self-instruction that I want to remember. A few years ago, I came up with the acronym and nonsense word, *E-TUG-OTH*, which stands for "Enjoy the Unique Gifts of This Hour." Another self-instructive wordplay I came up with is "Don't Let Your Blessings Turn into Burdens," which came to me as I realized I often get stressed out and feel burdened by things that are true gifts and blessings (entertaining, traveling, teaching, etc.)

- *Using one's preferred learning style* (more on this in a later chapter). Each of us has a preferred and stronger method of learning. It's important that we are aware of our strongest and preferred learning style and to use that with our spiritual learning. I prefer learning in a visual mode over an auditory mode, and I learn especially well when I use my mind to creatively manipulate the words or concepts.

From a Christian and spiritual standpoint, spiritual learning occurs and is effective when

- growth, learning, and maturity are *prayed about* on a regular basis;
- thoughts and questions are *shared with other Christians*;
- deliberate *prayers of thanks* are given *for insights and spiritual growth*; and
- *thanking God* at regular intervals *throughout the day*.

"Try It, You'll Like It!"—"He Likes It!"

After the airing and viewing of a 1972 commercial for Alka-Seltzer, the phrase, "Try it, you'll like it!" became popular. In another 1972 commercial, a big brother encourages Little Mikey, who doesn't like anything, to try Life Cereal. After Mikey eats some of the cereal, the older boy exclaims in surprise and amazement, "He likes it!"

I encourage you to try some of my ideas and methods. I truly believe you'll like them!

The reason behind my deciding to write is, I feel passionate about sharing with others the strategies and methods that have been effective for my spiritual growth, my learning to love God more deeply, and my improved relationship with Him. (And I continue to find these strategies helpful!) If my ideas help *at least one person*, my years of writing will be well worth it!

If you adopt on or two of these ideas, please commit to them for a period of three weeks to allow the activity to become a strong, solid habit and to bring about true change. Performing an activity sporadically a few times is not enough to form a habit as mentioned earlier. I urge you to try just one or two ideas at any given time—it was over several years that I adopted these new routines and habits, usually concentrating on one at a time. Also, please remember that we are all unique individuals and that different methods work for different people. If one strategy doesn't work for you, please try another one. I strongly believe that you, too, will find ways to feel closer to God, to experience a deeper peace and a more profound joy, accompanied by an overwhelming sense of gratitude! (I can say this so confidently *not* because they are my ideas but because they are based on scripture, on proven effective Christian habits, and on proven learning strategies.) I would like to strongly encourage you to use my strategies and principles but to *make them your own* by *using your goals and the methods that fit you best.*

My *spiritual quest* of desiring to grow spiritually and to learn to love God more completely has been—and continues to be—*an enlightening, exciting, rewarding, and fulfilling experience.* I invite you to embark upon your own spiritual quest and journey!

CHAPTER 3

Actively Learning to Love the Lord Thy God

*("with all your heart, with all your soul, with all
your mind and with all your strength")*

Defining "Love the Lord Thy God"

I realize that I've never been comfortable in expressing that I "love the Lord" or "love God." I've known that I am to worship God, obey God, serve God, revere, honor, and respect God…but it hasn't been in my practice to think or talk about *loving* God.

The word *love* is overused today, I believe, causing it to lose some of its significance. It also has more than one secular meaning in our society. We can *love* a sport, *love* our job, *love* chocolate or coffee, and also *love* our spouse and our family. I feel this makes the meaning of this verse more difficult to comprehend. I understand and frequently acknowledge love for my husband, children, grandchildren, and other family members, but how do I love God? Both parts of this verse, "Love the Lord thy God," and the latter part of the verse about loving God, "with all your heart, soul, mind, and strength," are hard for me to wrap my head around.

I contemplated the secular and biblical meanings of the words in the first part of the verse using a word-by-word approach.

A. Secular definitions of love

Dictionary definitions of *love* include:

- "an intense feeling of *deep affection*; a *great interest and pleasure* in something" (Google Dictionary)
- "*strong affection for another* arising out of *kinship* or *personal ties*"
- "warm *attachment, enthusiasm,* or *devotion*" (Merriam Webster)

The boldface phrases from the above definitions can have significance for how to love God.

- Loving God should be (with) intense feeling (i.e., "I should have interest and pleasure in loving God"; a strong affection out of personal ties should exist.
- With love, there should be an attachment (or connection), enthusiasm, and devotion.

A new definition of the word love

This quote from a marriage counselor referring to marital love is relevant (boldface and underlines added):

> It is time to change the meaning of the word "love." The word is mostly used according to the first definition given in the dictionary: "an intense feeling of deep affection."…After years spent speaking with couples before, during and after marriage… I am convinced of the partiality of the definition. **Love should be seen not as a feeling but as an enacted emotion. To love is to** feel and **act** lovingly." (Rabbi David Wolpe, *Time* magazine, Feb. 16, 2016, boldface added)

A major point of this book is that *our love for God needs to be shown in our actions*—it should be *enacted*.

B. My reflections about loving others

Trying to gain insight on what it means to love God, I reflected on what it means to me to love another person. In order to love someone, it is necessary

- to gain knowledge about that person, discovering their characteristics, who they are, their various roles, and what is important to them;
- to have knowledge about who I am so that I can share my innermost thoughts and dreams with that person;
- to give meaningful gifts to that person;
- to be fully accepting of the gifts they give to me;
- to be connected to them, to spend time with them;
- to derive pleasure, delight, and enjoyment from being with that person; and
- to make that person a priority.

The persons I love are always present in my mind to some degree, and my relationship with them directs a lot of my choices and activities. I believe that these same characteristics and the other qualities listed also apply to loving God.

- *Getting to know God.* In order to learn how to love God, I need to get to know God. I grew up in a minister's family, learning about God at an early age. I feel I have known about God for a long time, but my recent efforts to grow spiritually shed light on the fact that I need to continually learn about who God is as I change and age. In answer to the question "What does it mean to love God?", GotQuestions.org states, "First, *loving God requires knowing Him*, and that knowledge begins with His Word. It may sound glib, but *to know Him is to love Him.*"

- *Having knowledge of myself in relation to God and sharing my innermost dreams with Him.* The defining characteristic of God as our Heavenly Father also *defines who I am.* I am His child, loved by Him, in His care, and I know He has a plan for me. I've come to realize that among all the roles I have, *my most important role is as a child of God.*

- *Giving of myself, and other gifts, to God.* I believe that one of the best ways I can love God is by *surrendering* my will and trying to be open to His leading throughout the day.

- *Making it a top priority to spend time with God, to stay connected.* I am trying to spend time with God *first thing* every day, making it a priority to purposely pray and praise Him. I also know it is crucial to try to connect with Him numerous times throughout the day.

- *Allowing my thoughts, choices, and actions to be greatly impacted by my relationship with God.* When I have an awareness of His presence, my choices and actions are more likely to be aligned with His will. Thinking frequently about WWJD? (What would Jesus do?) can help keep me on the right track.

- *Fully accepting gifts from God.* I need to make it a point *every day* to *joyfully accept* His gifts to me, acknowledging who He is and who I am. Taking the time to mentally focus on receiving His love and on the fact that everything I have is a gift from God makes a big difference in my attitude.

C. Scriptural Foundations

In a sermon at church some years ago, Pastor Albert explained that there are four different words in the Bible which are all translated in our one word: *love*.

- The Greek word *eros* means "romantic love."
- *Storge* means "family love."
- *Philia* refers to love for other humans: care, respect, and compassion.
- *Agape*, the highest form of the four types, defines God's immeasurable, incomparable love for humankind. Agape love is divine love; it is perfect love, it is unconditional love, it is sacrificial love and pure love.

The above etymology of the word *love* lends insight to the command, "Love the Lord thy God." The biblical command refers not to romantic love or a familiar love or the care and respect we should show our fellow brothers and sisters. Since God loves us in an "agape way"—loving us with an unconditional, immeasurable, and incomparable love—we should attempt to love Him back in this same way. While we cannot achieve a pure and divine love, *I think the inclusive nature of this verse*, to "love God with all our heart, mind, soul, and strength" *indicates a comprehensive, sacrificial, and surrendering love.*

While considering what it means to love others can help give partial understanding of what it means to love God, it is important to realize that loving God is unique and different than loving others. Because God is divine, sacred, holy, perfect, all-powerful, and superior, loving Him needs to start by acknowledging all that He is. Loving Him should result in

- my worship of Him,
- my adoration of Him,

- my trusting in Him,
- my realizing He's in charge and in control,
- my respecting and honoring Him by aiming to become more obedient,
- my setting aside one day a week to worship Him in church, and
- my serving Him.

Significant facts about love *in the Bible*

We love because <u>he first loved us</u>. (1 John 4:19)

Beloved, let us love one another, for <u>love is from God</u>, and whoever loves has been born of God and knows God. (1 John 4:7)

<u>Put on love, which binds everything together</u> in perfect harmony. (Colossians 3:14)

<u>We know how much God loves us and we have put our trust in his love. God is love,</u> and all who live in love live in God, and God lives in them. (1 John 4:16)

Knowing these important biblical facts about love provides a background and a foundation on which we can love God and love others.

Spiritual Insights

The well-known Bible passage in 1 Corinthians 13 about love gives guidelines for loving others. I thought about the qualities of love in this passage in a new light, thinking about how they apply to loving God. The phrases "Love…rejoices in the truth," and "It

(Love)…always trusts," particularly spoke to me (1 Corinthians 13:6b, 7 NIV).

Do I *rejoice* in God's truths to me? I think I can show my love to God by rejoicing in the truths that I belong to, am loved by, am forgiven, and saved by God.

Do I *always trust* God? Too frequently I find myself worrying, stressing, feeling anxious, and wanting to control or fix a situation. I've decided that for me, totally trusting God may be *the hardest part of loving God.* I don't think I'm alone in the tendency to worry. Rick Warren has stated,

> **Worry may be the most common sin on the planet. It is the direct result of forgetting that God is good all the time.** ("Replace Worry with Worship," Daily Hope with Rick Warren, Feb. 27, 2019, LightSource.com, boldface added)

D. "Love the LORD": Secular and biblical definitions of the word *lord*

- "*a person who has authority*, control, or power *over others; a master*, chief, or ruler" (Dictionary.com)
- the meaning of *lord* in Hebrew—"sir, *master*, ruler, commander, possessor" (according to Google)
- "Lord is a title of respect…"; "Lord usually translates to *Adonai*, which is the equivalent of ruler or *master*; Lord usually translates to Yahweh (Jehovah), the sacred covenant name of God" (english.stackexchange.com)

In each of the definitions of the word lord *above, the word* master *is used.* We are instructed to love the Lord, our *Master.* The following quote, which includes both the words *master* and *Lord,* is relevant:

"Ye call me Master and Lord" (John 13:13)—but is He? The words **Master and Lord** have little place in our vocabulary, we prefer the words Savior, Sanctifier, Healer. **The only word to describe mastership in experience is love**...(*My Utmost for His Highest*, by Oswald Chambers, p. 266)

That quote was thought-provoking for me. Do I see the Lord as my master? As Chambers points out, *we prefer to see God "as our savior, sanctifier, healer" rather than as our master*. While Jesus *is* our savior, sanctifier, and healer, Chambers is pointing out that *Jesus asks us to also see Him as our master*.

There are numerous verses in the Bible with the phrase telling us to 'love the Lord.' According to answers.com, the phrase "love the Lord" is in the King James version of the Bible seventeen times. The phrase "fear the Lord" is found an additional twenty-seven times. According to Olive Tree Bible Software (blog), "Fearing the Lord means to be in awe of his holiness, to give him complete reverence and to honor him as the God of great glory, majesty, and power." It seems to me that "fearing the Lord" is related to *having Him as our master*: one who is our master is someone whom we hold in awe, to whom we owe complete reverence and honor, seeing His great glory, majesty, and power.

E. Conclusions about "loving the Lord"

The above quote from Chambers helped me see that loving God means not being selective about God's roles, that I shouldn't choose the characteristics I want God to have. Too often in the past I have viewed God's role as only the loving, giving Father, where *He does something for me*: He helps me, forgives me, comforts me, strengthens me, etc. If He is my master, *I need to also do something for Him*, I need to make the choice to serve him, to be submissive to Him, and to acknowledge that He is in control. God has given us the freedom to decide who or what will be our master. Chambers is saying *that to allow God to be my master is to love Him, and conversely, to love Him is to have Him be my master. This choice is crucial in determining the way we love God.*

F.   Definitions of *God* and *god*

Dictionary definitions of *God* are (underlines added):

- A being conceived as the *perfect, omnipotent, omni-scient originator and ruler of the universe*, the principal object of faith and worship in monotheistic religions (yourdictionary.com)
- In order to describe *God's attributes* or characteristics, theologians use three important terms: omnipotence, omniscience, and omnipresence" (study.com).
- "Omnibenevolent means all-loving. According to Christian teaching, *God proved his all-loving nature* by sacrificing his only son Jesus to make up for humankind's sins" (bbc.co.uk, "Nature of God in Christianity).

  With a lowercase *g*, *god* means "an object worshiped..." (Lexico.com).

G.   Meaning of "Love the Lord thy God"

This phrase, "Love the Lord thy God," is also found in several other verses in the Bible. Some of the additional verses are:

Be careful to observe the commandments
and **the law which Moses...commanded you,
to love the Lord your God...**(Joshua 22:5)

Take diligent heed to yourselves to **love the Lord your God**. (Joshua 23:11)

Love the Lord your God with all your heart and with all your soul, so that you may live. (Deuteronomy 30:6)

You shall therefore **love the Lord your God**…(Deuteronomy 11:1)

I found it noteworthy that not only do these verses tell us to love the "Lord thy God," but each of the verses above emphatically gives caution about the importance of doing so by using clear language: "be careful to," "take diligent heed to," "live so that you may," and "you shall."

Looking closer at the meaning of this phrase indicates a twofold meaning. The verse doesn't say just "love the Lord" or "love God" or "love the Lord God" but "love the Lord *thy God*." We are commanded

- *to love Him first and foremost, as a top priority*; and
- *to have no other gods*—to not *worship* family or personal goals or career or possessions or anything else. There should be no one or nothing that is the primary driving force or dominating focus of our thoughts other than God. If there is, then He is not our one and only God.

Reflections and soul-searching about "loving the Lord your God"

I reflected on: What/Who is a god to me? What/who do I truly *worship*? What do I value so much that it dominates most of my thoughts, desires, and actions?

Introspection indicated to me that family and personal goals can often be dominating and uppermost in my mind. I have read and learned that Christian service and aiming to *do things for God* can itself be a form of self-worship. All of the above can be a *god* to me.

While loving my family and wanting to do loving things for them and for God are not *wrong* goals, I must daily choose to *first seek God.*

This soul-searching about my priorities has led me to make it a point to try to apply "loving the Lord my God" to my daily life and to aim to always put God first. I feel an urgency about this—I need to do it *now*—not at some point in the future. *I need to choose to love God first now.*

Practical Ways I Can Attempt to Love God

I want to actively work on loving God more fully *today*. As I mentioned before, I am very aware of the need for daily periods of time alone with God and am disciplining myself to include those in my daily routine. Another goal has been to find ways to grow spiritually and to learn *to love God more fully within the framework of my daily schedule.*

The ACT2 Acronym

Referring back to the acronym ACT2, I list below some of the specific ways I've addressed the goals to grow and love God more fully within the framework of my everyday life and routines.

The *associations* for the first part of my morning routine are specifically directed to *first praising and worshiping God*, focusing my thoughts on His greatness. This is an important discipline for me, as my morning thoughts and prayers can easily be first focused on my agenda and myself. I try to remember *it's all about thee, not all about me.* The association of singing praise songs in my morning shower helps me to worship and praise him at the beginning of my day.

Associating thoughts about the nature of God as I stretch and lift up my hands in my morning exercises brings my mental focus *first to God's qualities as opposed to my desires or needs. I have changed and adapted the words to the praise song "Lord, I Lift Your Name on High" as I move and dwell on specific qualities of God.* The sequence of my morning exercises continues to be an association. After lifting and stretching up exercises, I next do stretches where I open my arms out wide, singing (out loud or mentally) my adapted words for "Open My Eyes That I May See," focusing on opening my mind, heart, and soul. I then bend to the floor and bow down low in an act of humility and servitude, and as I work on physical strength, I recite Bible verses that remind me that my strength is in the Lord.

Awareness—I'm disciplining myself to stop and to *be still for a few minutes every morning before I start the tasks of the day*. In these minutes, I aim to sense His presence and pray that I will be open to His leading.

Changes—*I give multiple daily prayers of thanks and gratitude*. A new habit or change during my day is that I stop to give prayers of thanks numerous times. In addition to trying to daily write in a gratitude journal, I now also take a moment several times to express my gratitude to God for the great, as well as small, blessings of that day. One reason I started this practice is due to a mental image I had one night based on the biblical story of the ten lepers. After being healed, they were so happy and excited, *yet only* one *of them went back to their healer to actually say thank you* (Luke 17:11–19). If I do nothing else worthy or important today, at least I will have genuinely thanked God for the blessings of this day.

Choices—*my attitude while working and/or doing chores*. I can choose to be grateful that I am able to work. I can view work and chores that I don't necessarily enjoy as opportunities for endurance and strength and growth in character. Choosing to keep things in perspective is helping me to let go of the feeling that my *project* or task is all-important.

Throughout—*reconnecting with God frequently* throughout the day. I am usually aware of the time, and I'm working on pausing mentally a few minutes at the start of every new hour wherever I may be. This is a challenge, as I so easily get caught up in the happenings of the day. This practice is in contrast to compartmentalizing my connectedness to God to specific, isolated time(s) and places.

Total—*Using more of my total being* in spiritual activities strengthens my connection with God, resulting in a closer relationship with Him: having a pen, paper, or highlighter with me to actively *write down* verses, thoughts, or questions related to my devotional reading; actually *kneeling down* to give prayers of gratitude makes a huge difference for me, *lifting up* my arms and hands with intercessory prayers as I lift up concerns for others or when lifting up praise and thanks to God, *opening up my hands* as I try to let go of cares and anxiety.

Words like *immersion*, *invasion*, *infusion*, and *flood* are descriptive of being *totally affected* by or overtaken. I love this song by Francesca Battistelli:

> Holy Spirit, You are welcome here
> Come *flood* this place and fill the atmosphere
> Your glory, God, is what our hearts long for
> *To be overcome* by Your presence, Lord.

In John Baillie's book, one of his prayers mentions the *invasion* of the Holy Spirit. I try to take a few minutes to focus on being totally impacted by God's presence—being flooded, invaded, and infused by His goodness, peace, and strength.

Concluding Thoughts on "Loving the Lord Thy God"

Using the acronym ACT again, I selected different words to help me remember some key points on *loving the Lord my God*.

I can AFFIRM God's love for me and affirm that I love Him. This daily affirmation is very powerful. Acknowledging that I am loved as a child of God and that He is in control elicits a *desire* to *love him*. I feel secure and calm in his love.

I can choose to be CONTENT. I sometimes have a mindset of wishing some things in my life were different while also knowing I have so much to be grateful for. A daily demonstration of my love for God can be my acceptance of what and where I am, consciously choosing a mindset of contentment.

I can TITHE some of my time, giving a portion of every day to God. One of my insights in this journey has been that I can give time to God in small periods of time throughout the day. Those minutes every hour (or maybe almost every hour) accumulate to be a significant portion of the day. I am not minimizing the need for an extended time of devotions and prayer.

Since loving someone results in having a relationship that is a *close, continual connection* with that person, I have found it helpful to substitute those words for the word *love* in this verse. I have paraphrased "Love the Lord thy God" with "Have a close, continual connection with the Lord thy God."

*****

In the next chapters, I share what I have learned about what it means to

- have a *close, continual connection* with the Lord thy God with all your heart;
- have a *close, continual connection* with the Lord thy God with all your soul;
- have a *close, continual connection* with the Lord thy God with all your mind; and
- have a *close, continual connection* with the Lord thy God with all your strength.

Practical ways that I can love God

- I can make a point to *love God fully today*. I can *focus on* being in a right relationship with Him and loving Him *right now*, this minute, this hour!
- The practice of memorizing hymn and praise song lyrics has resulted in changing my focus to God rather than on myself, my work, my family, etc.
- *Limit my caffeine intake*; too much caffeine results in the opposite of my being still, my being quiet, and my being able to focus on God.
- I need to *be open, have an open mind*. If a particular person pops into my head, I try to act immediately if I know that person is struggling in some way and make that phone call,

send that text or card, and say a prayer for that person. I so frequently ignore or put off those thoughts rather than follow through on them.

- Pause every hour to express my gratitude to God for all the blessings and help of the previous hour. After making it through a particularly difficult and demanding situation, I often sigh a sigh of relief, later realizing I never thanked God for following through on my earlier request to help me perform that task. One of my favorite passages in *Jesus Calling* is,

> Bring Me the gift of **thanksgiving,** which **opens your heart to rich communion with Me.** Because I am God, from whom all blessings flow, **thankfulness is the best way to draw near Me.** (June 25 selection, p. 184)

- I can *trust God* and *not worry*, remembering that He is God and I am not, that He is loving and the source of all good. I can be aware that I am stressing and worrying and then lift that concern in prayer and purposely change my thought to a positive one.
- I can be as *loving, kind, patient*, etc. as I can be *to those I am with today*.

I certainly am not great at following all these good intentions! But I am attempting to do them more often.

Multisensory and Multiple Intelligences Activities

As mentioned in the previous chapter about actively learning, we have preferred modes of learning and different types of intelligences. Howard Gardner proposed a model of different modalities of intelligence rather than seeing intelligence as a single general ability (*Frames of Mind*, 1983). Below are some suggestions for using

Gardner's modalities as a way to become more engaged in learning to love God:

- *Logical/Mathematical*

  Create a logical flow chart about loving God (a logical if…then series of thoughts) starting with "Because God first loved us…that means that He is…which leads to the fact that I should…"

- *Linguistic*

  Read a Psalm (perhaps Psalm 36:5a, 7a, 10) and then *write a Psalm of your own* expressing your love for God.

  - *Create an acrostic* that defines what it means to love God using words that begin with the letters of the word *love*.
  - *Write a letter to God* honestly telling Him how you feel and what you desire in terms of learning to love Him.

- *Musical*

  Sing a hymn or praise song out loud. (I especially like the simple song, "Father, I Adore You.")

  - *Compose your own song* or piece relating in some way to loving God.
  - Select a *Bible verse about loving God* and *put it to music*—either to the tune of a famous hymn or popular praise song or to your own tune.

- *Visual/Spatial (Artistic)*

  Draw, paint, or illustrate in some way a Bible verse about loving God.

- *Bodily-Kinesthetic*

  Add meaningful motions to a hymn or praise song as you sing it.

- *Naturalistic*

  Focus on any large or small item in nature, thinking of God's love for us and this world.

- *Interpersonal*

  Discuss and share with others what it means to love God in practical ways on a daily basis.

- *Intrapersonal*

  In an introspective way, *focus on God's love for you* and what that means in the way that you attempt to love God in return.

Ponderings and Quotes

(Questions and thoughts related to the topic of what it means to "love the Lord thy God")

- On the ThoughtCo website, Jack Zavada mentioned that "love as a word describes an emotion with vastly differing degrees of intensity."

  What or *who* do I love with the greatest intensity?

  Does the verse I am focusing on command us to love God with the *greatest intensity* of all people and things that we love?

  Can I truthfully say that I love God more intensely than anyone or anything else?

- It is a fact that *true love* for our spouses and other family members *grows deeper over time.* Is that happening with my love for God? *Is my love for Him growing and becoming deeper as I age and mature?*
- What *drives me*? What do I live for? Is my life purpose to have a loving relationship—a close, continual connection—with God?
- Can I say that I love God (or at least that I *aim and strive* to love God) in an "agape love" way—in a sacrificial, unconditional way? What do I sacrifice in order to love God?
- Do I primarily seek, desire, and pray for *God's blessings, or do I primarily seek his presence*? God instructs to seek *him.* The book *My Utmost for His Highest* by Oswald Chambers is considered to be the most beloved and popular devotional of all time. In this book, he states,

> We must not think about these (worldly) things… Whenever there is competition, **be sure that you put your relationship to God first."**

> <u>When we no longer seek</u> God for <u>His blessings, we have time to seek Him for Himself.</u>

While the following are *secular* quotes, they may shed some light onto what it means to love God.

> **Being deeply loved by someone gives you strength, while loving someone deeply gives you courage.** (Lao Tzu)
> (Do we gain *courage* by loving God?)

> **Love is like the wind, you can't see it but you can feel it.** (Nicholas Sparks, *A Walk to Remember*)
> (When/how/where/in what circumstances do I *feel* God's love?)

The opposite of love is not hate, it's indifference. The opposite of faith is not heresy, it's indifference, and the opposite of life is not death, it's indifference. (Elie Wiesel)

(How many of us as Christians are *indifferent* in how we feel about *loving God*?)

Love looks not with the eyes, but with the mind…(William Shakespeare)

(Am I loving God in a purposeful, MINDFUL way?)

Love never dies a natural death. It dies because we don't know how to replenish its source. (Anais Nin)

(How can we *replenish* our love for God?)

To love is to be vulnerable. (C. S. Lewis)

(Does our *vulnerability* have a role in our love for God?)

CHAPTER 4

Actively Learning to Love the Lord Thy God with All Your Heart

Defining Thoughts

The definitions of *heart* give insight while also raising some thought-provoking questions.

Secular meanings/associations with heart

Thinking of the heart organ in the body indicates its vital function: the heart is the essence of life, and it constantly pumps blood throughout our whole bodies, never stopping. The heart infuses the body with necessary energy, oxygen, etc., giving the body its life-blood. The whole body depends on the heart.

Google's definition of the heart is "the central or innermost part of something."

Another online site states that "the heart is compassion and understanding, life-giving and complex... Often known as the seat of emotions..." (umich.edu.symbolism>html>heart).

In our society, if something is dear to our heart, it is something that we are dedicated to and committed to; if something is on our heart, we are sincere about it and genuinely care about it.

These secular meanings consistently point to the essential nature of the heart. Reflecting on these can add some understanding to what it may mean to love God "with all your heart."

Scriptural Foundations

The Guideposts Family Concordance has served as a valuable resource for me in my research of the meaning of this verse. Its listing of words, definitions, and related verses has been very helpful in gaining insight into the specific verse I am seeking to understand.

What the heart is

An online site states that "the heart is that spiritual part of us where our emotions and desires dwell" (gotquestions.org).

The definition of *heart* from the Guideposts concordance states that in the Bible, the heart is seen as being "symbolic of intellectual, moral, and emotional functions of individuals; one's inner being."

I reflected on what my "intellectual, moral, and emotional functioning" says about my heart, my inner being, my core. Am I loving God from my core and inner being, intellectually, morally, and emotionally functioning and acting on loving God first?

The Guideposts Family Concordance lists verses including the word *heart*, organizing them according to the similarity of their meaning (pp. 317–318). These verses give a comprehensive picture of

- what is based in or seated in the heart,
- what actions God takes upon our hearts, and
- how we can respond with our hearts.

What is based in or seated in the heart?

The concordance lists several emotions that emanate from the heart, including *desire, fear, doubt, gladness, love, meditation, obedience, pride,* and *purpose* (p. 317).

Meditating on these emotions that emanate from the heart can be insightful into what it means to "love the Lord with all your heart." I gained some understanding by substituting the above emotions for the word *heart* in the phrase, "Love the Lord your God with all your heart."

- I am to love the Lord with all my *desire.*
- I am to love the Lord with (no) *fear.*
- I am to love the Lord with (no) *doubt.*
- I am to love the Lord with all my *gladness.*
- I am to love the Lord in all of my *meditation.*
- I am to love the Lord in being *obedient* in all things.
- I am to love the Lord with (no self-) *pride.*
- I am to love the Lord with all my *purpose.*

Making these word substitutions helped me to see some practical ways to work on loving God with all my heart.

What actions can God take on my heart?

"Loving God with all our heart" can be further understood by realizing that *God takes action upon our hearts.* It is because God works in our hearts that it is possible for us to fully love Him. I can gain understanding about loving Him by knowing what He will do for my heart if I believe and allow Him to do so.

- He *knows* our hearts (Psalm 44:21).
- He *searches* our hearts (1 Chronicles 28:9).
- He *enlightens* our hearts (2 Corinthians 4:6).

- He *opens* our hearts (Acts 16:4).
- He *recreates* our hearts (Ezekiel 11:14).
- He *examines* our hearts (Jeremiah 12:3).
- He *strengthens* our hearts (Psalm 27:14).
- He *establishes* our hearts (1 Thessalonians 3:13).

What are the results when God acts upon our hearts?

According to the Guideposts concordance, our hearts are regenerated by God. This regeneration or spiritual renewal results in our hearts being restored to the condition God intends. They will be:

> clean, enlightened, joyful in God, meditative, perfect, prayerful, pure, glad and sincere, and wise. (p. 317)

Wow! All those actions are so uplifting and encouraging!

How are we to respond with our hearts?

The concordance gives additional depth of understanding about loving God with all our hearts by listing the *responses brought by a renewed and regenerated heart*. We are to respond by

- *believing with* our hearts (Romans 10:10).
- *sanctifying God* in our hearts (1 Peter 3:15).
- *doing God's will* from our hearts (Ephesians 6:6).
- *serving God* with all our hearts (Deuteronomy 26:16).
- *walking before God* with all our hearts (1 Kings 2:4).
- *trusting the Lord* with all our hearts (Proverbs 3:5) (p. 317).

Below are what kind of place our hearts should be, according to the Bible:

The heart is a place where God dwells.

- "Christ may dwell in your heart" (Ephesians 3:17).
- "God in your heart" (1 Peter 3:15)

The heart is a place with singing and rejoicing.

- "Singing with grace in your heart" (Colossians 3:16)
- "My heart rejoiceth in the Lord" (1 Samuel 2:1).

The heart is a place that is not hardened.

- "Harden not your heart" (Hebrews 7:8, 4:7).

The heart is a place defined by what is treasured most.

- "Where your treasure is, there will your heart be also" (Matthew 6:21).

The heart is a place that is true with a single intention.

- "Draw near with a true heart" (Hebrews 10:22).
- "Singleness of heart" (Colossians 3:22)

The heart is a place filled with light.

- "Our hearts flooded with light" (Ephesians 1:16).

All of the above qualities indicating what God intends for our hearts lend insight to what it means to "love God with all your heart." Our hearts should be a place where God resides, therefore a place that is full of light, joy, and singing. Our heart is a place that can be molded and changed. Our hearts will hold what we value and treasure most (and spend most of our thoughts and time on). Basically, I think these verses tell us that we need to *give our hearts completely to Him.*

Other verses referring to "all your heart" or "whole heart"

In addition to the verse focused on in this book, there are other verses that specifically give a directive to do something with *all your heart* or with *your whole heart*. These verses give added insight about what God intends us to do with our whole hearts.

> Serve Him with all your heart… (Deuteronomy 11:13)

> Happy are those who…who seek him with their whole heart…(Psalm 119:2)

> "If you seek me with all your heart, I will let you find me," says the Lord…(Jeremiah 28:13–14)

> That I may keep your law and observe it with my whole heart. (Psalm 119:34)

> Trust in the Lord with all your heart. (Proverbs 3:5)

> And serve Him with wholehearted devotion and with a willing mind…(1 Chronicles 28:9)

Some well-known Bible verses are about the heart

While doing this research, it occurred to me that some of the most well-known and most-often memorized Bible verses have to do with the heart.

> Create in me a clean heart, O God…(Psalm 51:10)

> Let not your heart be troubled…(John 14:1)

> Blessed are the pure in heart. (Matthew 5:8)

I believe it is significant that this verse instructs us to love God with all our hearts. Loving God with all our hearts is at the center and core of our faith and relationship with God.

Henri Nouwen's writing adds insight into the heart

A few years ago, I picked up devotional booklet by the internationally renowned priest and author, Henri Nouwen (Returning to God, A Lenten Journey with Henri J.M. Nouwen). I found several quotes referring to the heart and our relationship with God.

We need to have a **change of heart**. (p. 3)

Jesus asks us to **move our hearts to the center, to have as our priority a heart set on a spiritual life, the center of all we think, say, do.** (p. 1)

God says, "Turn around, **set your heart on my kingdom**. I give you all the freedom you desire." (p. 15)

Let my love touch the deepest, most hidden **corners of your heart.** (p. 8)

Where are our hearts? **When we worry, our hearts are in the wrong place.** (p. 4)

Often my heart is drawn to my own worthless treasures. (p. 12)

Prayer is seeking our home where the Lord has built a home—in the intimacy of **our** own **hearts."** (pg. 13)

Conclusion

I reflected on what it means to "love the Lord your God with all your heart" or to love God *wholeheartedly*. It seems obvious that this means to love God with one's whole being, with all one's feeling and passion, and with true sincerity. Synonyms of *wholeheartedly* include "deeply, earnestly, from the bottom of one's heart, genuinely, in all sincerity, profoundly, really, true, without equivocation" (from Google's online definition).

In contrast, *half-hearted* (from Google's online definition) is defined as "without enthusiasm, apathetic, cool, impassive, indifferent, lukewarm, neutral, spiritless, tepid."

Some thought-provoking questions

- I feel this verse tells us to love God in a way that is not half-hearted and not in a lukewarm manner. Do I do that? *Do I love God with 100 percent of my being and in a way that is not just lukewarm?*
- The heart is also considered to be the source of one's desires, passions, and yearnings. *Do I have a desire, a passion, and a yearning for loving the Lord?* The first step in loving Him is to *want* and *desire* to love the Lord with all my heart.
- To love God with all my heart also implies that I love Him *more* than anyone or anything else. *Does my love for God have first, second, or third place compared to other persons or other things in my life?*
- Thinking about loving God with all my heart motivates me to want a pure and clean heart, a heart that is open to receive his love, and a heart that is right in God's sight. *Do I have the right priorities of heart, the right passions? What am I really worshiping? Am I worshiping God or my desires, my plans, my dreams for what I want to do and be?*

I believe that filling my heart with adoration and worship for God will result in a heart that is more pure—a heart that is how God intended it to be.

What does it mean in practical terms in everyday life to love the Lord wholeheartedly?

- As I mentioned earlier, loving God with my whole heart and with my whole being means that *I need to be actively involved, focused, and engaged in my relationship with God.*
- *I need to make loving God* with my whole heart *a daily goal* and *my aim in life.*
- *To receive His love requires focus, quietness, and stillness. I need to carve out some time out of each day to be quiet and still when I can focus on accepting God's love for me.* I am intellectually aware of God's love for me, but I need to act on this knowledge again and again. *Every day I need to open my heart, receive His love, and acknowledge it.*
- Once I acknowledge and receive God's love for me, I can begin to love Him more fully. I have found that there is a reciprocal nature of loving God with all my heart: as I am open to receive God's love, *the next step is for me to affirm that I do love Him, thus giving Him my love*, and then I can begin to love others. In this process of first receiving and then giving, I end up *receiving* love back again. This is a constant process of *giving* and *receiving*, an ebb and flow.
- I need *humility.* To truly love God with my whole heart, I must be humble, seeing my weakness in comparison to His strength and omnipotence. *Humility leads to being dependent and reliant on Him.*

Conclusions about loving God with all my heart

In the previous chapter, I substituted descriptive words for loving someone for the word *love* in the verse that is the focus of this book. I paraphrased the verse to say, "Have a close, continual connection with the Lord your God…"

If I use that same strategy and substitute words defining *heart* into the verse, the paraphrased verse becomes: "Have a close, continual connection with the Lord your God with all your being, from your center and your core, and with all your passion…"

This act of paraphrasing and substituting defining words into the verse gave me some personal insight and depth of meaning.

Benefits of aiming to love God with my whole heart

- I have discovered and experienced great *benefits* from aiming to love God with my whole heart! When this is my focus, *I feel secure in His love, which results in deep joy.*
- If I concentrate on being *fully filled* with His love, *I become satisfied, content, and fulfilled.* As I aim to return God's love for me, *I feel a sense of purpose* and direction.
- My *priorities will be right if loving God becomes foremost,* with all other things secondary. Believing and *feeling that my priorities are right gives me a sense of calm, security, and confidence.*

Using the ACT2 acronym

Below are some of the ways that I apply the actions of this acronym to loving God with all my heart:

Associations—Whenever I think of one whom I hold close to my heart, I can make a quick association with my love for God, reminding myself to love God first and foremost and also that God loves my family member more than I do.

Awareness—It is well known that strengthening our core leads to improved balance and stability. I can *have a heightened awareness of my core* when I exercise and, throughout the day, realizing on how central it is to my overall health. *I can be aware of how crucial it is to love God from my core and center of myself.*

Change—The phrase "change of heart" can be used to remind myself to change the focus of my love and passion to loving God with all my heart.

Choices—If I acknowledge His love for me and *if I love God in return with my whole heart*, the choices I make of *what I eat and drink, what I do, and how I do* are all impacted by a desire to do what's healthy and honorable to my body, to others, and to God.

Throughout—Just as *my heart pumps blood throughout my body*, I can think about how *my love for God should permeate my whole being and my whole day.*

Total—Thinking of the contrast between doing something wholeheartedly compared to half-heartedly reminds me to *reflect daily on whether or not I am loving God with all my heart, with its totality.* Sometimes my heart isn't in reading devotions or doing a particular task. I need to bring my focus back to the right priorities.

A new ACT acronym

Summarizing what I have learned about loving God with all my heart, I used the acronym ACT with words relating to my heart. *Loving Him with all my heart* means that

- I express *adoration* for Him and worship Him from my heart;
- I focus on being *centered* and grounded by having loving God as my purpose; and
- I *thank* God from the bottom of my heart, acknowledging that all good things come from Him.

Multisensory and Multiple Intelligences Activities

Logical/mathematical

Work on *memorizing numbers of certain Bible qualities*. Use those numbers when aiming *to remember those specific qualities*. For example, there are sixteen characteristics of love in 1 Corinthians 13:4–9, fruits of the Spirit (Galatians 5:22–23), and there are seven to nine gifts of the Spirit (depending on the source you use).

Linguistic

- *Write a passionate prayer or letter* to God.
- *Write a love poem* (while at first that sounded sacrilegious to me, I realized that the Psalms as well as many hymns and praise songs are basically love poems).
- *Write a poem or statements of adoration and worship.*
- *Form an acrostic* using the first letters of the word *heart*.
- *Read out loud, using feeling and passion*, a psalm, a prayer, your own writing.

Musical

- *Passionately sing a Bible verse or poem* about loving with all your heart using a well-known praise song or hymn melody.
- *Compose a tune/melody/musical composition* that passionately expresses your feeling about loving God with your heart using words or with no words.

Visual/spatial (artistic)

- *Illustrate the verse, "Make love your aim,"* or another verse about passionately loving God with your heart.
- Make a symbolic *illustration of the heart of a tree or a plant* (see idea under "Naturalistic" below) and relate it to loving God from our innermost part, etc.

Bodily kinesthetic

- *Move/create motions/act out/choreograph* exercise routines or sacred dance to The Lord's Prayer or a Psalm or verses about loving God with all our heart.
- Assume a *posture that is humbling, reverent, submissive*, etc., such as kneeling at bedside, bowing down, lying prostrate on the floor, or bowing head and folding hands, or postures that are *lifting up, opening up*, etc. as you focus on loving God with all your heart.

Naturalistic

- *Think of "hearts" in plants/trees*, etc. such as hearts of celery, hearts of romaine, the heart of a tree, etc. and how they can be an example of our center and core and to our loving God with all our hearts.

Interpersonal

- *Share and discuss with others* what circumstances/situations, etc. elicit a passionate feeling for God. How do you express your love for God in a passionate way? How do you feel you can grow in loving God with all your heart?

Intrapersonal

- Analyze and *reflect on what things have helped you feel a deeper love toward a family member* (e.g., the passage of time, shared experiences, etc.). Then see if you can *relate some or all of those ways to loving God with more of your heart.*

Ponderings and Quotes

- "*A listening heart is always open* and sensitive to the joy and pain of others, offering a space within itself for the other to enter..." (Eliezer Shore in "Friends of Silence," Vol. XXX, No. 3).

  (Can I be more loving to God by having a heart that is more open to others' joy and pain?)
- From Mark Nichol, online, some "heart idioms" give further insight into the heart:
    - *wholeheartedly*—with complete sincerity and *commitment*
    - the *heart of the matter*—the essence, the core
    - from the *bottom/depths of one's heart*—profoundly
    - with all one's heart—with great enthusiasm

How can these idioms help in understanding what it means to love God with all our hearts?

The following quotes were found on goodreads.com:

And now here is my secret, a very simple secret: It is only with the heart that one can see rightly; what is essential is invisible to the eye. (Antoine de Saint-Exupery, The Little Prince)

It is better in prayer to have a heart without words than words without a heart. (Mahatma Gandhi)

One love, one heart, one destiny. (Robert Marley)

The heart has its reasons which reason knows not. (Blaise Pascal)

The following are from brainyquote.com:

The best and most beautiful things in the world cannot be seen or even touched—they must be felt with the heart. (Helen Keller)

For in the dew of little things the heart finds it morning and is refreshed. (Kahlil Gibran)

If you carry joy in your heart, you can heal any moment. (Carlos Santana)

C H A P T E R   5

Actively Learning to Love the Lord Thy God with All Your Soul

Defining Thoughts

Of the four ways we are commanded to love God, the most obscure in my mind is loving God with all my soul. I feel I have a good comprehension of what my heart, mind, and strength are, thereby having a better knowledge of what it may mean to love God with all my heart, mind, and strength. My understanding of the word *soul* is somewhat vague and unclear.

Secular Meanings and Use of the Word *Soul*

The following quote points out the vagueness of the word *soul* in our society:

> The word "soul" can often feel like a nebulous word in English, it doesn't always communicate what it means. Soul has been coined in jazz and blues music, and it's used to describe a certain kind of southern comfort food. But is this the same "soul" we read about in scripture?" (firmisrael.org)

Other secular phrases which may add to either the understanding or confusion about *soul* are references to a person being a "lost soul" or being "the life and soul of the party," a "kind-hearted soul," or a "soul sister" or "soul brother." We can "bare our soul," do some "soul-searching," or "sell our soul to the devil."

Some formal definitions of "soul" are: "<u>...the spirit and essence of a person</u>...the part of you that makes you who you are and that will live on after your death...<u>the part of you that will go to heaven and be immortal, according to the teachings of certain religions.</u>" (yourdictionary.com)

<u>The part of you that consists of your mind, character, thoughts, and feelings</u>... (Collinsdictionary.com)

Scriptural Foundations

The Hebrew translation for *soul* has multiple uses and meanings in the Bible, which translate to numerous words in English. Perhaps this adds to the misunderstanding or confusion about what the soul is. "The Hebrew word *nephesh* generally translates to "soul." *Nephesh* is also translated in English as *"living being, life, creature, mind, desires, heart, appetite, persons..."* (firmisrael.org).

The soul is basically our mind, our emotions, and our will. It is who we are as human beings. (Christianity.com)

It (the soul) speaks of the very essence of a person. (firmisrael.org)

> The real you, which is your soul and
> what you think…(Robert McLaughlin, Bible
> Ministries on gbible.org)

The definitions cited above point out the similarity in religious and secular meanings. The idea that one's soul determines one's thoughts, one's will, one's choices, and, therefore, one's character, making a person who s/he really is, are components of both religious and secular meanings. However, the biblical perspective adds this crucial difference:

> The soul is a gift from God to glorify God…
> the purpose of the soul that God gave you: (is) to
> bring glory to Him through submitting to His
> will and commands…(Robert McLaughlin, gbi-
> ble.org)

> Bless the Lord, O my soul; and all that is
> within me, bless his holy name. (Psalm 103:1)

Additional understanding of the Christian viewpoint of *soul* can be found in other Bible verses and biblical references.

The Guideposts Family Concordance (p. 665) states that one's soul

- belongs to God, and
- is our most vital asset.

> What good will it be for someone to gain the
> whole world, yet forfeit their soul? Or what can
> anyone give in exchange for their soul? (Matthew
> 16:26)

> In addition to the biblical command to
> love the Lord with our soul, the Concordance
> also states that other duties of the soul are to

seek, thirst after and desire and serve the Lord. (Guideposts Family Concordance, p. 665)

The Lord is good unto them that wait for him, to the soul that seeketh him. (Lamentations 3:25 KJV)

As the deer pants for streams of water, <u>so my soul pants for you, my</u> God. <u>My soul thirsts for God,</u> for the living God. When can I go and meet with God? (Psalm 42:1–2 NIV)

You, God, are my God, <u>earnestly I seek you; I thirst for you, my whole being longs for you</u>… (Psalm 63:1)

But <u>be very careful to keep the commandment</u> and the law…to love the Lord your God… to hold fast to him <u>and to serve him with all your heart and with all your soul</u>. (Joshua 22:5)

Psalm 119 uses these words relating to actions of the soul: "My soul…longs for…clings to…treasures…loves…delights in…"
There are numerous Bible verses about *God dwelling in us and abiding in us.* Is the soul the place of *indwelling?* Can I love God with all my soul by acknowledging that He dwells in my soul?

All who keep his commandments abide in him, and he in us. And by this we know that he abides in us, by the spirit which he has given us. (1 John 3:24)

The Divine Indwelling: The Spirit of God within…animates our existence at every moment. We know this by faith. ("Contemplative Life

Program, Welcoming Prayer, Consent on the Go," p. 8)

The quotes and verse below indicate that we need to choose and give consent.

> The indwelling Spirit calls us to wholeness… <u>All that is required is our consent…to continually turn and return to the indwelling Spirit of God in faith and trust.</u> ("Contemplative Life Program, Welcoming Prayer, Consent on the Go," p. 13–14)

The chorus of the song "Holy Spirit" by Francesca Battistelli is especially relevant.

> Holy Spirit, You are welcome here
> Come flood this place
> And fill the atmosphere
> Your glory, God,
> Is what our hearts long for
> To be overcome
> By Your presence, Lord.

It is important to take the time *now*, this minute, to respond to God's Spirit in our souls.

> Think of the things that take you out of abiding in Christ—"Yes, Lord, just a minute… when this week is over, I will abide then"… <u>Begin to abide *now*…</u>" (*My Utmost for His Highest*, O. Chambers, p. 166)

We are also instructed to give all of ourselves to God, including giving our souls to Him.

> Submit yourselves therefore to God... (James 4:7 NIV)

> Give yourself completely to God—every part of you...to be tools in the hands of God, to be used for his good purposes. (Romans 6:13)

> Let me then put back into Thine hand all that Thou hast given me, dedicating to Thy service all the powers of my mind and body...(and I think we can also add the word *soul*). (*A Diary of Private Prayer* by John Baillie, p. 13)

Spiritual Insights

Definitions of *soul* indicate that the soul is the *essence* of a person that which makes each of us who we are as unique individuals. The soul refers to our will and our purpose. The biblical understanding of the soul tells us that our souls belong to God and that we should submit our wills to Him. The purpose of our being and the purpose of our lives—which is seated and based in our souls—is to bring glory to Him, to serve Him, to love Him, and to obey Him. Since we are instructed to love God with all our soul, we are to love Him with the essence of who we truly are. We are to love Him in our thoughts, in our will, and in our choices.

The meanings of *heart* and *soul* are similar in that both the heart and the soul are referred to as our core and innermost part. I think that the use of both *heart* and *soul* in this verse can be viewed as a powerful and repetitive emphasis in this command to love Him from our core, from our center, and with the essence of who we are.

Another perspective on what it means "to love the Lord thy God with all your soul" can be gained from an online article, which focused on this great commandment:

> This is a love that takes over everything! It is a love expressed with "…the sincerity of the soul…" (firmisrael.org)

Another site points out the difference between loving with our heart and our soul in this way:

> We love with (our) heart—with affection, and we love with (our) soul—with devotion." (GregSimas.org)

To love the Lord with all my soul means to love Him in the way I live, in the choices I make, and in the behavior and lifestyle I adopt. It has to start from *within*. If I love God with all my soul, my love for God defines *who I am*, my love for God dominates my inner being, and my love for God directs all my actions. I think that loving the Lord with all my soul means giving Him consent to abide in my soul, to submit myself and my will—daily rededicating my soul to Him.

But *how* do I know that I am doing that *daily*? After reflecting on this, I came to the conclusion that I need to start by acknowledging that my soul belongs to God. Loving God with all my soul, with all my being, entails acknowledging that I do not *own* my soul. I must spend quiet time with Him, focusing on giving my soul to Him by emptying my mind, my will, and my soul of selfish desires so that He can cleanse and fill my soul with His Spirit. This is hard for me to comprehend, yet I know and have the faith that it is true—that Christ and His Holy Spirt can dwell in me, in my soul. Loving God with all my soul means aiming to let Him dwell, abide, and fill my soul.

This awareness can be achieved by stopping activity and through stillness, silence, and meditation. I can find God, feel His presence and His gifts deep inside my core, in my soul. If I focus on His gifts, I will receive them, including His peace and His joy. He is there, but

I need to *stop*, be *still*, be *silent*, and *seek* Him. Therefore, I think that part of loving God with all my soul requires that I spend some time in solitude, being *still* and silent, to quiet my soul, connect with God and hear His voice.

> Be still and know that I am God. (Psalm 46:10)

The quotes below speak to this:

> When I fail to embrace the solitude of God's peace, I get caught up in the **world's downward spiral** of violence and turmoil… Solitude plucks us out of the world's frenzy and **centers** us in nonviolence. Solitude silences the loud voices within us to allow the still, small voice of God to speak. Solitude gives God the time and space to disarm our inner wars and gives us the strength to receive God's gift of peace, and **to learn to be at peace** with ourselves and those around us. (*Living Peace* by John Dear, in "Friends of Silence, Feb. 2017, emphasis added)

> Listen in the silence for Spirit's voice
> guiding your soul…
> Listen, attune, and heed the inner Voice of Love.
> For in sacred Silence, we **open ourselves**
> To Wisdom,
> To **ever deepening communion with**
> **The Source of all creation.** (*Lumen Christi…*
> *Holy Wisdom* by Nan Merrill in Friends of
> Silence, March 2017)

Another way that I can begin to love the Lord with all my soul is to "empty my soul." My soul must be emptied of *impurities* so that there is ample room to be filled with the life-giving force given by God's Spirit. I often get consumed and filled up with worry and stress, wishing I could change a situation, etc. This "clogs up" my channel to peace, as my connectedness with God is not clear. On page 107 of *Jesus Calling*, Sarah Young says, "When things go wrong, your trust-flow slows down and solidifies."

Kenneth Copeland explains his visual imagery about God's power being available to him through a pipe.

> I saw a pipe stretching between God and myself. The pipe was a funnel for the power of God. At God's end, there was a surge of power going in. At my end, there was only a trickle flowing out. The pipe was clogged with dirt and filth…the filth was unforgiveness and had been put in the pipe (my spirit) one grain at a time. God was not holding back His power… The pipe was so clogged that His power could not flow through it. (*Walking in the Realm of the Miraculous*, pp. 61–62)

Loving God with all our souls means having an open, free-flowing connection with Him—having a soul that is *empty* and ready to be filled. Listening to Sound of Life Radio one day, I heard Doug Hannah say, "The hole in our souls is shaped like a cross. Only God can fill our souls."

We are told that we can be filled with the Holy Spirit, "But be filled with the Spirit" (Ephesians 5:18) and that we can gain strength from Him, "On the other hand, I am filled with power, with the Spirit of the Lord" (Micah 3:8).

I believe that loving God with all my soul also means having a *well-nourished* soul, since He wouldn't want my soul to be *undernourished* or *unhealthy*. After thinking about what "feeds my soul," I came to the following conclusions:

- Expressing gratitude to God *feeds* my soul.
- Serving and helping others in Christ's name feeds my soul.
- Engaging in worship feeds my soul.
- Listening to music can feed my soul.

- Loving God with all my soul requires more than the crucial acts of being still. I need to respond to God's actions upon my soul by expressing my gratitude to Him, by worshiping Him, and by loving and serving others.

Educational Principles

After using the methods of studying, doing research, meditating and journaling to try to learn what it means to love God with all my soul, I focus next on applying this knowledge to my daily personal life. What are some practical applications of what it may mean to love God with all my soul? I have found that the following practical methods are helpful to me.

- Making it a daily routine and habit to be still for a period of time—to open my soul while breathing deeply and focusing on being filled—is crucial, as mentioned above.
- I know that it is also important to engage my brain by memorizing specific verses relating to the soul. (It is easy to do a Google search to find verses relating to any specific topic.)
- Also, I can incorporate the learning principles of repetition and practice on a daily basis to strengthen knowledge and habits, which encourage a connection with God.
- I can creatively express thoughts about my soul and about loving the Lord with all my soul.

Some specific routines that I use are listed below, once again using the ACT acronym to make them easier to remember.

Daily Activities Using the ACT2 Acronym

Associations

I can associate deep breathing exercises with my soul being filled with the Holy Spirit. I meditate on being filled with His presence as

I inhale and an emptying of worldly or selfish desires as I exhale. I do this exercise daily in my morning time of sitting and being still.

In the morning, as I apply makeup, curl my hair, etc., I have made the association, so I focus on my soul and try to achieve a "quiet and gentle spirit" as I silently recite this verse: "Rather let your adornment be the <u>inner self</u> with the lasting beauty of <u>a quiet and gentle spirit,</u> which is very precious in God's sight" (1 Peter 3:4b).

Aware(ness)

Having an ever-present awareness of all the ongoing small and large blessings and gifts from God, remembering that all good things come from God, and remembering all the answered prayers instill a deep sense of gratitude. I am trying to remember to say a prayer of thanks with every new hour throughout the day.

Frequently directing my mind to focus on God's qualities of being omnipotent, omniscient, and omnipresent brings me a strong awareness of His power as evidenced in nature, His trustworthiness because He is all-knowing and loving, and His presence with me always. Being aware of these qualities has great impact on my soul.

Change

Loving God with all my soul means acknowledging that my soul belongs to Him and that if I submit my will (my soul) to Him, He will change and transform me according to His will. I am aiming to be open to His will and change in me with every new hour in the day after I give a prayer of thanks.

> Positive volition in the soul is everything. <u>When that positive volition is there, God will mold the pot into an honorable vessel of mercy.</u>
> (Robert McLaughlin, gbible.org)

> For it is God who is at work in you, enabling you both to will and to work for his good pleasure. (Philippians 2:13)

Choice

I have a choice between just thinking about being grateful or acting upon that thought by actually getting on my knees or taking a few minutes to write that prayer of gratitude. A more sincere and soul-felt prayer results when I am more engaged. It really doesn't take that long to either kneel privately or to jot down a prayer, but I have found that these choices give me a more soul-felt connection.

Throughout

It helps me to focus on adverbs meaning *throughout*, which I've come across in reading various devotionals to describe a Spirit-filled soul: the soul is invaded, infused, flooded, permeated, infiltrated, saturated, immersed, soaked. I try to create a mental image of these words for how the filling of my soul can impact me throughout my whole being.

As mentioned above, I am working on remembering to take a few minutes at the change of every new hour *throughout the day* to give thanks, to sense His presence, and to be open to His leading.

Total

Some phrases using the root word *total* are "totally awesome," "totally committed," "totally devoted," among others. If I acknowledge that our God is totally awesome, I should be totally committed and totally devoted to Him. These are ways that I can love Him with all my soul.

The words listed above for *throughout* are also applicable for the concept of *total*.

As for some ideas for using the ACT acronym specifically for the soul, I came up with the words **A**llow, **C**entered, **T**hink.

I need to *allow* God to take over my soul and acknowledge that it belongs to Him. As Oswald Chambers says, "Our salvation is not earned, it is accepted" (*My Utmost for His Highest*, p. 343).

I need to be open and welcome Him into my soul, to give consent to His abiding presence. Another quote that speaks to this is: "There is Good News! The indwelling Spirit calls us to wholeness in, with, and through the human condition. All that is required is our consent" (*Welcoming Prayer: Consent on the Go*, p. 13).

I need to be *centered* in Him. "Being centered means that you have a reference point or a place to come back to when life's challenges and emotions push you off balance" (psychologytoday.com).

I *think* about and meditate on the fact that since my soul belongs to God, therefore my will belongs to God. I aim to follow His leading in my next actions.

This quote from Soren Kierkegaard addresses this: "I found I had less and less to say, until finally, I became silent and began to listen. I discovered in the silence the voice of God."

Multisensory and Multiple Intelligences Activities

Logical/mathematical

Using reason and logical thinking, what can you/we infer about our souls based on what we know about God and His characteristics and the fact that we are made in His image?

Linguistic

Focus on *words* that describe a *filling* of our *souls* and contemplate on what fills your soul…and what do you want your soul to be filled with? If we do want to love God with all our soul and to be filled with the Holy Spirit in my *soul,* are we experiencing it to the degree these words describe? Are we

- infused
- permeated

- ingrained
- throughout
- flooded
- invaded by/invasion
- soaked in
- immersed in
- inseparable
- absorbed by
- obsessed with
- indwelling
- abiding
- penetrating
- infiltration
- all-encompassing

Journaling—whether it be prayer journaling or other journaling—is/can be a *baring of the soul.*

Think about the fact that it is the same root to both the word *journey* and *journal.* How can journaling help in a spiritual growth journey?

Write a prayer/poem/lyrics for a song focusing on all you have to be grateful for. *Gratitude feeds and fills the soul!*

Study a passage or book from the Bible, praying for enlightenment before reading, underlining, highlighting, writing questions, doing research using a Bible commentary. This is a way to *have the word of the Lord dwell in your soul!* (How can Jesus's words dwell and abide in me unless I read and memorize scripture?)

Musical

Read the quotes below and then choose a piece of music to listen to, really feeling it in your *soul.*

> Music is to the soul what words are to the
> mind. (Anon)

> Where words fail, music speaks. (Hans Christian Andersen)

> There's nothing like Music to relieve the soul and uplift it. (Micky Hart)

Another way to memorize scripture is to memorize hymn and praise lyrics, as almost all of them are based on a Bible verse. It's easier to remember the words when you sing them! (This is a proven learning strategy.) This is *a way to fill our souls and minds with the right things.*

- Sing the hymn "Be Still and Know That I Am God."
- Sing the praise song "Bless the Lord."
- Memorize and sing the hymn "How Great Thou Art."

(Feeling close to nature brings us close to God...*being outside, experiencing nature, can feed our souls.*)

> O Lord my God, when I in awesome wonder,
> Consider all the works thy hands have made,
> I see the stars, I hear the mighty thunder,
> Thy power throughout the universe displayed.
>
> Refrain:
>
> Then sings my soul, my Savior God, to thee;
> How great thou art, how great thou art!
> Then sings my soul, my Savior God, to thee:
> How great thou art, how great thou art!
>
> When through the woods and forest glades I
>   wander
> And hear the birds sing sweetly in the trees,
> When I look down from lofty mountain grandeur,
> And hear the brook and feel the gentle breeze.

And when I think that God, his Son not sparing,
Sent him to die, I scarce can take it in,
That on the cross, my burden gladly bearing,
He bled and died to take away my sin.

When Christ shall come with shout of acclamation
And take me home, what joy shall fill my heart!
Then I shall bow in humble adoration, and there
    proclaim,
"My God, how great thou art."

Visual/spatial (artistic)

Illustrate/draw a symbol for your soul. I drew an illustration for
soul as a *spiral coil*, open and moving upward within me. A spiral coil
is *open* and becomes increasingly wider and more open as it reaches
higher up.

Draw/illustrate/paint images of ways to refresh your soul, feed
your soul, etc.

Choose a Bible verse about *soul* that is significant to you and
write it in calligraphy.

Draw or sketch a glass as an analogy of the soul (the soul is like
a vessel to be filled). Illustrate various steps or conditions of getting
a glass filled with water and relate it to having your soul filled by the
Holy Spirit. For example, first, the glass needs to be clean before it is
filled; second, one must ask for the water; next, the glass needs to be
empty before it can be filled. The glass needs to be still—not moving
all around—so that it can be filled. Write/draw or meditate on how
these steps and conditions can relate to having your soul *filled.*

Bodily-kinesthetic

Contemplating on my soul made me think of my diaphragm—
is this where we can think of the soul as being housed? If we think of
the soul as being our innermost part and core, then the diaphragm
could correspond anatomically. When thinking of the diaphragm, I

think of the act of breathing. I can choose to connect to and be aware of my soul as I focus on my breathing. A deep breath, which is then released slowly while mentally letting go of stressors, is a relaxing technique with many physical and mental and spiritual benefits.

Breathing is an important aspect of meditation, and meditation is a way of connecting to our souls. We can work on this practice through meditation and deep breathing while at the same time

- being cognizant of and aware of your connection to your soul with each breath;
- being aware of God's presence inside of you;
- focusing on a desire to breathe in what's clean and pure as you inhale, filling and opening up your soul to God's presence as your diaphragm expands; and
- focusing on breathing out the impurities (the earthly concerns that can fill us up) as you exhale deeply.

Breathing is the very essence of life, and the soul is the very essence of one's being. As regular, healthy breathing is essential to our physical lives, the health of our souls is essential to our spiritual wellness. The breathing process of filling up or inhaling, followed by an emptying out or exhaling, can be analogous to the necessary emptying and filling up of our souls. As you take deep breaths, say (or meditate upon) the following:

- "I can breathe in *faith* and breathe out *fear.*"
- "I can breathe in *patience* and breathe out *pettiness* and *pride.*"
- "I can breathe in *humility* and breathe out *haughtiness* or a holier-than-thou attitude."
- "I can breathe in *renewal* and breathe out *resentment.*"
- "I can breathe in joyful *anticipation* (of healing, etc.) and breathe out *anxiety.*"

I remember my dad sharing with me a deep breathing exercise that he would often do, which I have found to be very effective:

while inhaling deeply, followed by slowly exhaling, think or say the following:

> Every day, every hour, Father,
> I breathe in Your gracious power:
> The power to love, the power to be pure,
> The power to be strong, the power to endure.

Engage in *physical motions* and *movements* such as *lifting up* arms and hands with lifting up thoughts to God, using your arms to *push out* any negativity, *opening up hands* in release, giving control to God.

Naturalistic

Contemplate the spiritual *analogies* of various elements of weather: the breeze or wind as a descriptor for the Holy Spirit, thinking of having your soul filled by the Holy Spirit.

Think of the breeze as the "breath of God," perhaps singing to yourself the hymn "Breathe on Me, Breath of God" while focusing on your soul being cleansed and then filled.

Interpersonal

Consider "baring your soul" to a family member or close friend, sharing with him/her about any aspect of the soul—what you have found to refresh, feed, or speak to your soul, etc., Then ask them to bare their soul and share with you, if they feel comfortable doing so. We can learn and gain so much from what strategies work for others.

Intrapersonal

Read and reflect on some of the Bible verses and/or quotes and questions relating to *soul* in the *ponderings* section at the end of this chapter. What can you learn about yourself and your soul that you weren't previously cognizant of?

Below are some Bible verses about the soul:

The Lord is good unto them that wait for him, to the SOUL that seeketh him. (Lamentations 3:25–26)

Teach me the way I should go, for to you I lift up my soul. (Psalm 143:8)

When the cares of my heart are many, your consolations cheer my soul. (Psalm 94:19)

But if from there you seek the Lord you God, you will find him if you seek him with all your heart and with all your soul. (Deuteronomy 4:29)

Truly my soul finds rest in God; my salvation comes from him. (Psalm 62:1)

Why, my soul, are you downcast? Why o disturbed within me? Put your hope in God… (Psalm 42:11)

This is what the Lord says: "Stand at the crossroads and look…ask where the good way is, and walk in it, and you will find rest for your souls…" (Jeremiah 6:16)

Praise the Lord, my soul; all my inmost being, praise his holy name. (Psalm 103:1)

The law of the Lord is perfect, refreshing the soul. (Psalm 19:7a)

But be very careful to keep the commandment and the law that Moses…gave you: to love the Lord your God, to walk in obedience to him, to keep his commands, to hold fast to him and to serve him with all your heart and with all our soul. (Joshua 22:5)

You know with all your heart and soul that not one of all the good promises the Lord your God gave you has failed. Every promise has been fulfilled; not one has failed. (Joshua 23:14)

Ponderings and Quotes

Consider the order of the phrases in this well-known verse: "He maketh me to lie down in green pastures; he leadeth me beside the still waters. He restores my soul…" (Psalm 23:2–3a KJV).

Is it significant that preceding the phrase, "he restores my soul," are the phrases, "lie down in green pastures" and "beside the still waters"? Do the choices we can make of lying down to rest and being outside in calming places play a role in the restoration of our souls?

What is a soul? It's like electricity—we don't really know what it is, but it's a force that can light a room. (Ray Charles)

Hope is the thing with feathers that perches in the soul…(Emily Dickinson)

Faith and prayer are the vitamins of the soul; man cannot live in health without them. (Mahalia Jackson)

Permanence, perseverance and persistence in spite of all obstacles, discouragements, and impossibilities: It is this, that in all things distinguishes the strong soul from the weak. (Thomas Carlyle)

Happiness resides not in possessions, and not in gold, happiness dwells in the soul. (Democritus)

Music washes away from the soul the dust of everyday life. (Berthold Auerbach)

To be rooted is perhaps the most important and least recognized need of the human soul. (Simone Weil)

Food for the body is not enough. There must be food for the soul. (Dorothy Day)

The aim and final end of all music should be none other than the glory of God and the refreshment of the soul. (Johann Sebastian Bach)

CHAPTER 6

Actively Learning to Love the Lord Thy God with All Your Mind

The dictionary definitions and synonyms below have helped to clarify what it means to love God with all my mind.

> The mind is "the...part...that reasons, thinks, feels, wills, perceives, judges, etc." (Thesaurus.com)

Synonyms for *mind* include "...proclivity, intent" (Thesaurus.com), with *proclivity* defined as "a tendency to choose or do something regularly; an inclination or predisposition toward a particular thing" (Google dictionary).

Based on the above definitions, loving God with all my mind means to deliberately choose and have the will to love God on a regular basis. If I have the intent, the tendency, and the practice to choose to love God frequently, loving God will then become a natural inclination and predisposition.

Spiritual Foundations

By gaining a deeper understanding about what the Bible says about the mind, I can have insight about how to love God with all my mind. The Guideposts Family Concordance defines the *mind* as "the reasoning facility of an individual; memory; intention" (p. 451).

As in the above definition, *intention* is used, indicating that to love God with all my *intention* means I deliberately place loving Him as my primary aim and goal. I have the ability to choose the direction of my thoughts, and I think loving God with all my mind means mentally focusing on my relationship with Him.

Bible verses listed in the concordance give additional perspective on the biblical meaning of *mind*. On page 451, the "mind" is referred to as being *regenerative*: it has the capability of being spiritually reformed or reborn. The following verse gives a directive that we should renew our minds: "Do not conform to the pattern of this world, but <u>be transformed by the renewing of your mind</u>" (Romans 12:2a).

As Christians, we are to renew and redirect our aims and goals so that we are intentional, willful, and consciously deliberate about loving God first. Our motivations should not be for short-lived worldly goals but rather for eternal qualities. The Bible tells us that the purposes for which we are made are to love God first, love Him more than anything else, and give Him glory. I believe that to "renew our minds" means to redirect and change our mental focus back to this mindset of loving God first, and that in this way we can love God with all our minds.

The second part of this verse goes on to say, "Then you will be able to test and approve what God's will is…" (Romans 12:2b).

I love the promise of this verse, as I often struggle with discernment of God's will. If I aim to renew my mind—making my purpose loving God rather than conforming to worldly goals—then I will be able to "test and approve what God's will is." As I focus more on loving God, I believe that I will have a better awareness of God's will.

At the same time, negative actions of the mind need to be avoided so that we can more fully love God. Numerous verses in both the Old Testament and the New Testament instruct us not to worry. One of the most famous verses about worry is Jesus telling us, "And don't be concerned about what to eat and what to drink. Don't worry about such things" (Luke 12:29 NLT).

After analyzing my thoughts over a period of time, I realized that a great percentage of my thinking is consumed by worrying and fretting! I've found Rick Warren's writings on the topic of worry very helpful.

> Worry is a sign that you're trying to be God. The greatest stress reliever to me is this sentence: God is God, and I'm not.
>
> Worry is the warning light that shows I've stopped looking to God to meet my needs.
>
> Worry is really just a form of atheism. Every time you worry, you're acting like an atheist. You're saying, "It all depends on me." That's just not in the Bible. (Rick Warren quotes about *worry* on A-Z Quotes)

The Bible points out other common pitfalls we need to be aware of as Christians: disunity and disagreement among ourselves and attitudes of haughtiness.

> I plead with Euodia and I plead with Syntyche to <u>be of the same mind in the Lord</u>. (Philippians 4:2 NIV)

> <u>Be of the same mind toward one another; do not be haughty in mind</u>, but associate with the lowly. (Romans 12:16 NASB)

The verses and insights from the concordance emphasize the importance of having my mind *right* in God's sight: being renewed to focus on loving Him, being free from worry and disunity with others, and not having a haughty attitude. If my will and intention is to love God before all else, I will have a better understanding of His will and, therefore, will be able to love Him with all my mind.

Conclusion

The biblical and secular definitions of *mind* tell us that our minds determine our will, our intentions, and our primary purpose in life. Because we are able to direct our thoughts, loving God with all my mind means that I need to choose to mentally focus on and give top priority to my relationship with Him and on things that make a difference for eternity. Focusing on God's greatness and goodness and acknowledging that He is in control should result in my mind being at peace as opposed to being filled with worry. I should have the mindset of working harmoniously with others without an attitude or haughtiness. These are all ways that I can aim to love God with all my mind.

Retraining My Brain to Focus More on Him
Ways I Can Direct My Thinking toward Loving God

I have learned that *I can retrain my brain* to associate God's presence by making associations between my daily routine and my surroundings with His qualities, His gifts, and His presence. I can practice being more aware of what is going on in my mind. I can choose what fills my mind and occupies my thoughts. I can purposely direct my thinking from negative to positive thoughts.

A few years ago, the *New York Times* Sunday magazine showed a diagram of a human head and brain using a pie graph to depict amounts of thinking devoted to various topics. This visual image spurred me on to reflect on what most of my thinking is devoted to. I determined that my thinking is usually devoted to one of my roles: as a wife, a mom, a grandma, a teacher, a friend, etc. It occurred to me that I have another role: that of being a child of God. I rarely focused on that role, yet that is clearly the most important role that I have.

I can choose to direct my thoughts to this role. Since I am a child of God, He loves me and plans good things for me and my family. By thinking about God's goodness and generosity, His power and His perfection, I become aware of all that I am lacking. This leads me to the realization that I need to rely and depend on Him. This "reliance mindset" leads me to acknowledge all that He has given me, which results in a feeling of indebtedness and sincere gratitude for all He is and all He does.

I have found that the mental work of memorizing Bible verses and passages, together with hymn and praise song lyrics, is vital to filling my mind with the right thoughts. These memorizations provide an *arsenal* of positive thoughts that I can refer to. They replace negative, worrisome, stressful, and anxiety-ridden thoughts that often pop into my mind. In the past, I felt that it would be effective to say to myself, "That is a negative thought—let it go get rid of it." I believed that being aware of and desiring to let go of a negative thought would allow me to move to a positive mindset. That is easier said than done! My mind frequently circles back to ruminating on fretful, worrisome thoughts.

An effective strategy for me has been to immediately start reciting a verse or singing a hymn or praise song—either silently or out loud. This brings a change to my perspective and moves my thoughts in a positive direction. The negative thoughts no longer dominate my thinking! I call this Thought Replacement Therapy. The verse and lyrics bring my mind back to God's greatness, His love, His control, His grace, etc. This results in the situation and my problem not seeming so important as I lift my thoughts outside of myself and up to Him.

I call this practice Thought Replacement Therapy. When I am dwelling on a negative thought or a situation, I start reciting a verse or lyrics to a praise song or hymn. Not only does this change my mind's focus to another topic, but it also changes my perspective and my attitude. The lyrics/verse(s) bring my mind back to God's greatness, His love, His control, and His grace. My situation and my problem are no longer so important, as my thoughts are lifted up to Him and His greatness and away from my earthly concern.

Colossians 3:2 says, "And set your minds and keep them set on what is above, not on the things that are on the earth." Joyce Meyer refers to this verse in her book, stating, "We can have right and wrong mind-sets. The right ones benefit us, and the wrong ones hurt us and hinder our progress. With God's help we can set our minds in the right direction" (*Closer to God Each Day*, p. 33).

By thinking about God's goodness and generosity, His power and perfection, I become aware of my weakness in contrast to His strength. This leads me to a realization that I need to rely and depend on Him. This "reliance mindset" leads me to acknowledge all that He has given me, which results in a feeling of indebtedness. I can train my brain to frequently or always *have an attitude of gratitude*. When I acknowledge His love, when I choose to believe that all things will work out for good for those who love Him as He has promised, *when I realize His greatness and my smallness and adapt an attitude of gratitude and humility, I feel amazing therapeutic effects*! Thinking about God's qualities, His gifts, His greatness, His majesty, all He has created, His omnipresence, etc. leads to a desire to *give Him praise and thanks*.

Desiring and Expecting to Learn and to Have a Close Relationship with God

I need to desire a close relationship with God. As mentioned above, I need to have the mindset, the goal, and the intention of loving God. Every day, I must choose to love God and to love Him more than anyone or anything else.

I need to have a mind that is *ready* to learn before I read a passage of scripture or a devotional. In the past, I would not always engage my mind when I read the Bible or a devotional book. I have found it helpful to get a pen and paper and to then write down verses that "speak to me." If nothing speaks to me, then I either reread the passage or keep reading. It seems to almost be a waste of time if I am not impacted or changed in some way by what I have read. In *Closer to God Each Day*, Joyce Meyer refers to Acts 17:11, "They received the word with all readiness of mind, and searched the scriptures daily…" She goes on to say, "The Bible says that we are to have a ready mind. That means we can have minds that are open to the will of God for us…" (p. 38).

I need to truly believe that I can be filled with the His Spirit. While I've heard and *known* most of my life that we as Christians can be filled with the Holy Spirit, it is a difficult concept for me to grasp. I know that I need to grow and believe more deeply that I can actually be filled with His Spirit. I have learned that I need to have an open mind, a mind that is receptive and welcoming to the Holy Spirit in order to have a close relationship with God.

I need to sense His presence with me. With deep breathing and a mental focus on His characteristics and gifts, I can sense His presence. I have learned that the gifts of peace, joy, and love and God's presence are always available, but that I must make the choice to stop, to be still, and to open my mind so that I can access and receive them. I also am working on listening to and acting upon "that still voice," that niggling thought to do something, to make that phone call, etc.

Meditating on a close relationship with God led me to contemplate the opposite of a close relationship. A relationship that is not close is defined by feelings of distance and separation. In my experience, the following states of mind lead to a feeling of separation and distance from God:

- worry, stress, anxiety;
- thinking that I am in control;
- feeling a sense of entitlement and/or discontent or disappointment;
- getting too caught up in my *worldly* responsibilities and obligations, being too caught up in myself, making myself too important;
- depending on other things or other people rather than depending on God;
- putting myself, my agenda, my work, or my projects first rather than putting God first; and not trusting Him.

If I love God with all my mind and if I aim to align my mind with His will, then I believe that

- I will be able to think more clearly, positively, and confidently. I will have more clarity for decisions with the right priorities and the right perspective. When I have the right priorities, I will be able to do more of what really matters in life.
- trying to align my thoughts with God's will and acknowledging that He is in control leads to an attitude of "let go

and let God." As a result, I end up worrying and stressing less and am more energetic and efficient. If I love God with all my mind, I will not overthink things but instead will have a childlike *trust* in Him.

- when I put loving God first, I have less discontent and feel more at peace. I realize that what is of most value is to feel connected to God, to enjoy the gifts of this day, and to be loving to others. Nothing else really matters!

Educational Principles

Having a mindset of a student. I have come to the conclusion that learning to love God with all my mind is a journey that must be made step-by-step, that I'm not there yet, and that I never will perfectly achieve this goal. I have found the saying, "Progress, not perfection" (from Alcoholics Anonymous), to be encouraging. I wish that I could do everything that I have learned and that I have written about in this book, but I acknowledge humbly that it is a constant challenge to put into practice the habits and changes I strongly believe in. I know that I have to keep working at it and that hopefully I am moving in the right direction and making some progress daily.

Using Visual Imagery and Other Strategies to Keep Focused

I find that even when I sing or read out loud, my mind can still wander some and not be totally focused on what I am singing or reading. It has helped me greatly to use visual imagery. I form a mental picture of the words, perhaps also creating a setting to correlate with the words or with the *mood* of the music.

I also will frequently substitute my own words, to elaborate upon the given words and ideas. In this way, I am focusing and engaging my mind on my feelings, my desires or spiritual goals, which results in a heartfelt, sincere, and personal expression to God. My mind does not wander when I employ these mentally engaging strategies.

Using the ACT2 Acronym

Association(s)

I can associate a visual image of clouds with my thoughts and just let any negative thoughts drift by.

Awareness

I can have an awareness of what my thoughts are, what they are focusing on, and then consciously change them if they are not positive, constructive thoughts.

Change

I can "change my mind" in a positive direction to be more aligned with His will with His help—"Be transformed by the renewing of your mind" (Romans 12:2).

I have changed my devotional habit by readying my mind to learn and be impacted by what I read. Having a pen and paper with me as I read encourages me to write down and aim to remember part of what I read.

Choices

We have free will to make choices using our minds throughout every part of every day, and I can aim to align my will and all my choices, great or small, with God's will.

Throughout

Throughout the day, aiming to do this at the change of every new hour, I can fill my mind with sincere gratitude and thanks, mentally singing praise songs and hymns or reciting a Bible verse.

Total

I can aim to focus my total mind—my thinking, my feeling, my sensing, and my intuiting—on God, His goodness, His love, and loving Him in return (the four aspects of consciousness according to C. G. Jung. Google.com).

Using a New ACT Acronym for Loving God with All My Mind

Affirm that I am a child of God. If I affirm—that is, if I state as a fact and assert strongly—that I am a child of God and that He loves me, my perspective and my priorities change for the better!

Concentrate on making it "*not* all about *me* but all about *thee*." Specifically, I can focus on God's attributes (His omnipotence, His omniscience, His omnipresence, His omnibenevolence); I can focus on worshiping Him right now; I can focus on giving gratitude right now for all His gifts; I can focus on *glorifying* Him right now and on what it may mean to glorify Him; I can focus on my role as a child of God rather than focusing on my other earthly roles.

Think about "whatever is true, whatever is noble, whatever is right, whatever is pure, whatever is lovely, whatever is admirable, if anything is excellent or praiseworthy, think about such things" (Philippians 4:8 NIV).

Multisensory and Multiple Intelligence Activities

Logistical/mathematical

Write a logical flow chart about how being a child of God can impact my thinking: "*If* I am first and foremost a child of God, *then* it naturally flows that I will..."

Explore what it may mean to love God with all the aspects of your brain. (The different functions of the parts of the brain are personality, thinking, planning, problem-solving, speech, hearing, movement, memory, sight, smell, balance, and others.)

Spatial/visual

Use the *Da Vinci doodling technique* to think about and expand upon a spiritual goal or spiritual truth.

Draw a sketch of a human brain and draw a pie chart inside of it. Section off the pie chart to depict different percentages of topics your thoughts are devoted to, such as work, family, God, money/financial, etc. Try to come up with ways that you can focus more of your thinking on God.

Linguistic

Create anagrams and/or other "word plays" to help memorize goals, remember importance points, etc. For example, I made up the following anagram to help me focus on living in the present:

E TUG OTH, which stands for Enjoy the Unique Gifts of This Hour. I sometimes find myself either wishing for a time in the past or for a time in the future, and remembering this anagram helps me to focus on the gifts of the moment.

Use a journal to write prayers, thoughts, and insights related to a devotional reading or scripture passage.

Read or recite a prayer, a devotional, a Psalm, or other scripture passage out loud, putting emotion and feeling into your reading.

Write about a spiritual gift using the "stream of consciousness" method.

Study a book in the Bible as you would study other content areas: highlight, write, and reflect on it; use a commentary; and read a book that has been written about it.

Musical

Sing a praise song or hymn either out loud or mentally.

Memorize a Bible verse and then put it to the tune of a well-known praise song or hymn.

Visually imagine the concepts, words, and ideas in that verse.

Interpersonal

Discuss with others a devotional book or other faith-based book.

Share with a close friend what you feel you spend most of mental energy on and listen to their ideas on the same topic. Brainstorm together as to how you can devote more of your mind and thinking to God.

Intrapersonal

Meditate on one of the spiritual gifts or fruits of the SPIRIT listed in the Bible.

Reflect upon which spiritual gift or spiritual fruit is a weak area for you and which gift or fruit you feel is an area of strength. Brainstorm ways you could develop and grow in the area in which you feel weak.

Reflect on how you can use the ACT2 acronym: (making) *associations*, (having more) *awareness*, (making a) *change*, (making different) *choices throughout* (the day) and (with 100 percent) *total* (effort) to loving God with all your mind.

Naturalistic

Memorize a verse or verses for various parts of nature such as the sky, wind, grass, flowers, etc., and when you are outside, focus your mind on that verse/those verses, bringing a biblical perspective to mind.

Engage your mind by doing some research to learn about a particular plant, type of rock, species of animal, etc. Think about how awesome our Creator is!

View items in nature with a *new* perspective, a new sense of awe and appreciation for the patterns, intricacies, microscopic detail, immense grandeur, etc. of all of nature.

Bodily/kinesthetic

Assume postures of humility, reverence, and servitude when you pray, when you mentally focus on God's greatness, and when you think about aiming to serve God. For example, kneel at your bedside, bow down, lie prostrate, or get in the yoga child's pose.

Put specific motions to a verse, hymn, or praise song and do theses motions while reciting or singing. For example, every morning, I go through an exercise and stretching routine of lifting up my arms and hands (and also simultaneously doing various leg exercises) as I sing several verses of "Lord, I Lift Your Name on High," opening my arms up and out (while doing a different leg exercise) as I sing "Open My Eyes That I May See."

Additional Bible Verses Related to the Mind

Set your mind on things above, not on earthly things. (Colossians 3:22 NIV)

The human mind plans the way, but the Lord directs the steps. (Proverbs 16:7)

If any of you lacks wisdom, you should ask God, who gives generously to all...(James 1:5 NIV)

The fear of the Lord is the beginning of wisdom; all those who practice it have a good understanding. (Psalm 111:10)

Your attitude should be the same as that of Christ Jesus…taking the very nature of a servant…(Philippians 2:5–7)

They received the word with all readiness of mind, and searched the scriptures daily…(Acts 17:11)

But the wisdom from above is first pure, then peaceable, gentle, open to reason, full of mercy, and good fruits, without uncertainty or insincerity. (James 2:17)

Finally, beloved, whatever is true, whatever is honorable, whatever is just, whatever is pure, whatever is pleasing, whatever is commendable, if there is any excellence and anything worthy of praise, think about these things. (Philippians 4:8)

Ponderings and Quotes

Our life is shaped by our mind; we become what we think. Joy follows a pure thought like a shadow that never leaves. (Buddha)

You have power over your mind, not outside events. Realize this, and you will find strength. (Marcus Aurelius)

Do not dwell in the past, do not dream of the future, concentrate the mind on the present moment. (Buddha)

I found that when you start **thinking** and **saying** what you really want, then your mind automatically **shifts** and **pulls** you in that direction. (Jim Rohn, iamfearlesssoul.com)

In solitude the mind gains strength and learns to lean upon itself. (Laurence Sterne)

All things that truly matter, beauty, love, creativity, joy and inner peace arise from beyond the mind. (Eckhart Tolle)

To understand the immeasurable, the mind must be extraordinarily quiet, still. (Jiddu Krishnamurti)

Life isn't as serious as the mind makes it out to be. (Eckhart Tolle)

The primary cause for unhappiness is never the situation but thought about it. Be aware of the thoughts you are thinking…(Eckhart Tolle)

People are just as happy as they make up their minds to be. (Abraham Lincoln)

What does it mean to glorify God? I came up with ways I feel I can glorify God and formed the acronym GTP2—Gratitude, Trust, Praise, Prayer.

My gratitude acknowledges that all good things come from Him, my trust acknowledges that I know He is in control, my praise acknowledges that He is worthy of praise, my prayer acknowledges that I want to be close and connected to Him.

CHAPTER 7

Actively Learning to Love the Lord Thy God with All Your Strength

Defining Thoughts

Since some versions of this verse use the word *might* and some use the word *strength*, I looked into the meaning of both words. *Merriam-Webster* defines strength as the "capacity for exertion or endurance." To that definition, dictionary.com gives second and third definitions as "(2) mental power, force, or vigor; (3) moral power, firmness, or courage."

The second definition of *might* in *Merriam-Webster* includes "the power, energy, or intensity of which one is capable."

I can substitute the definitions for the word *strength* and ask myself, "Am I loving God with all my mental power, force, and vigor? How much energy do I exert in loving God? Do I love God with all my power?"

Spiritual Foundations

While the meanings of *strength* and *might* seem obvious, it is significant to know that the Bible tells us in numerous places that the source of our strength is from God, Christ, and the Holy Spirit.

> He gives power to the weak and strength to
> the powerless. (Isaiah 40:29)

For the joy of the Lord is your strength. (Nehemiah 8:10)

The Lord is my strength and my song... (Exodus 15:2)

The Lord, the Lord, is my strength...(Isaiah 12:2)

But those who trust in the Lord will find new strength. They will soar high on wings like eagles. They will run and not grow weary. (Isaiah 40:29)

And the God of all grace...will himself restore you and make you strong...(1 Peter 5:10)

I can do all this through him who gives me strength. (Philippians 4:13)

But the Lord is faithful, and he will strengthen you...(2 Thessalonians 3:3)

Look to the Lord and strength...(1 Chronicles 16:11)

The Sovereign Lord is my strength... (Habakkuk 3:19)

The Lord gives strength to his people... (Psalm 29:11)

God is our refuge and strength, an ever-present help in trouble. (Psalm 46:1)

The Guideposts Family Concordance gives the simple definition of *strength* as "power" (p. 683), and the word *might* is defined as "effective power" (p. 449). Various verses are listed under the following headings to indicate that there are different types of might: God's; man's physical; man's intellectual and moral; and man's spiritual (might) coming from God, Christ, and the (Holy) Spirit.

The concordance also lists verses telling us that the way to gain an *increase of strength* is (p. 683)

- from God

    "For I am your God. I will strengthen you and help you" (Isaiah 41:10).

- from Christ

    "But the Lord stood at my side and gave me strength…" (2 Timothy 4:17).

- from His Spirit

    "I pray that from his glorious, unlimited resources he will empower you with inner strength through his Spirit" (Ephesians 3:16 NLT).

- from (our) brothers (in Christ)

    "But I have prayed for you, Simon…and when you have turned back, strengthen your brothers" (Luke 22:32 NIV).

- (through) Wisdom

    "Wisdom gives strength to the wise man more than ten rulers who are in a city" (Ecclesiastes 7:19 ESV).

- (through) Waiting on the Lord

  "But they that wait upon the Lord shall renew their strength; they shall mount up with wings as eagles; they shall run and not be weary; and they shall walk, and not faint" (Isaiah 40:31 KJV).

- (through) Lord's grace

  "And he said unto me, My grace is sufficient for thee: for my strength is made perfect in weakness" (2 Corinthians 12:9 KJV).

Loving God with All Our "Muchness"

Looking to the Hebrew meaning of the word gave profound meaning and insight to this part of the verse. Kevin Burns explains that

> The Hebrew word for *strength* used in this verse is "me'od."… It is typically translated "very" or "much"… It is not physical strength. The word conveys the idea of not a thing in particular, buy everything in general. It is every possibility, opportunity, ability, and capacity you possess. It is not a thing, but everything. Love God with everything… Jesus said "mind and power" in Mark 12. These words help unpack the meaning. All of our human capacities can be used to love God and neighbor. Everything, every moment, every opportunity, every ability can be used to love the honor the One who made us. (https:/kevinburns2019.sqyarespace.com/home/loving-god-with-your-muchness)

The choice of the words *throughout* and *total* in my acronym ACT2 tie in closely with this concept of loving God with all my "muchness." As I have pointed out, I have come to the conclusion that I need to work on loving God throughout my entire day and with total energy and commitment in all I do.

Spiritual Insights

What can these verses about looking to God for our strength and growing and increasing our strength from God tell me about loving God with all my strength?

The message I gain is that because I need the Lord is the source for strength, I can love Him more fully by looking to Him, waiting on Him, leaning on Him, relying on Him, and knowing that my strength can be increased by Him. Because these are ways that create a closer relationship with Him, a deeper and stronger love for Him will result.

These verses also indicate that all components of our triune God are sources of strength: God our Father, Jesus Christ, and the Holy Spirit. I should regularly access and feel the blessings of His strength through all of His forms. Also, the Bible tells me that the church and other Christians are sources of strength to me, as I can be a source of strength to my brothers and sisters in Christ. These truths indicate to me that I can love God with all my strength by being closely connected to the Father, the Son, and the Holy Spirit and by being an active part of a church, through which I can gain and give support and strength.

Wisdom is also mentioned in the above verses. Through the regular practices of studying, praying, meditating on God's Word, and praying for wisdom, I can love Him with more of my strength.

To love the Lord thy God with all my strength or might also means

- to love Him in an active, mature way.
- to love Him in a way that is not weak.
- to acknowledge that I am weak compared to His strength.

- to make loving Him a major focus every day.

  Strength implies health, growth, and maturity. Therefore, to grow stronger in my faith and in my relationship with God is a way to love Him with all my strength. As I age, I don't want to grow bitter, resentful, angry, or be consumed by worry. Instead, as I become older, I want to grow stronger the way God wants me to—to grow stronger in grace, to grow stronger in gratitude, to grow stronger in love. These are ways that I can love God with all my strength.

  I also realize that I need to *act* and not just sit passively, expecting God to change me. I need to do certain things that are in my control in order to allow God to work in me. It's crucial that I take the time to read His Word, to study His Word, to memorize His Word; to meditate; to stop, be still, and listen to His voice; to act upon that subconscious voice in my head saying to do or not to do something. I need to slow down and be more mindful. I need to put God first throughout the day, I need to make a decision to go to church and worship Him on Sundays. These are some of the decisions I can make in order to let the Holy Spirit work in me and which will result in my loving Him in a stronger way.

- Loving God with all my strength means loving Him with full commitment and with full enthusiasm, as opposed to loving Him in a lukewarm or apathetic way.

  I know that this takes a purposeful decision, time, work, and effort.

- I can only love God with all my strength if I acknowledge my weakness and then become reliant on Him.

  The Bible states that we receive God's strength in the areas of our weakness, "Likewise the Spirit helps us in our weakness…" (Romans 8:26).

I like this quote from Oswald Chambers, "Complete weakness and dependence will always be the occasion for the Spirit of God to manifest His power" (*My Utmost for His Highest*, p. 126).

In order to love God with all my strength, I need to acknowledge that it is by God's grace that I receive strength from Him. I must admit my weakness, surrender my will and my desire to control situations to Him, and instead rely on Him. The importance and effectiveness of reliance on God is found numerous times in the Bible.

> And the men of Judah were victorious **because they relied on the Lord**, the God of their fathers" (2 Chronicles 13:18b).

> Then Asa called to the Lord his God and said "Lord there is no one like you to help the powerless against the mighty. Help us, O Lord our God, **for we rely on you. O Lord**, you are our God. (2 Chronicles 14:11)

Relying on God and trusting in Him are basically the same. I feel that by practicing to trust God more often in more areas of my life, my trust in God is growing. I can love God with more strength, as my trust in Him grows stronger.

If I turn to God in my weakness, "my weakness can be wonderful!" Some days when I have felt my worst, I have prayed for help to make it through just a small part of the day at a time. I continued to pray for the next small part and the next and the next…and literally "prayed my way through the day." Later, I realized how that day turned into a really good day because of my reliance on God's help each step of the way. On days when I feel well physically and feel confident and strong, I often do not pray or seek God's guidance, instead relying on my own strength, often straying off in a wrong direction, ending up with a not-so-good day.

Loving God with all my strength means having a major focus on loving Him. Choosing to have the priority of loving God and focusing on loving God needs to be a daily choice.

I meditated on what it means to fully rely on God, to give up my self-reliance by surrendering to Him. I came up with the following ideas:

- I can stop trying to change things that I cannot change and instead be at peace with myself, my circumstances, and with God. I have come to realize that feelings of discontent and disappointment can be a result of wanting to control everything rather than accepting that God is in control. Surrendering my desire for controlling everything leads to acceptance of the way things are, acknowledging that God has it all under control.

- I need to give up *earthly* desires and temptations such as what I want for myself, for my family, for my career, and even for this book project. I need to surrender all my cares, all my worries, all my burdens. A benefit of surrendering is that I receive His gifts once I give up my will to Him—I receive His peace, His joy, and His strength when I have surrendered my cares and burdens. When I am filled up with stress, worry, and trying to control certain situations, I am not free to receive God's gifts.

> Submit yourselves therefore to God… Draw
> near to the Lord, and He will draw near to you.
> (James 4:7–8)

> Give yourselves completely to God—every
> part of you…to be tools in the hands of God, to
> be used for his good purposes. (Romans 6:13b)

Educational Principles/Practical Applications

Using the ACT2 acronym

Associations. I have made associations between certain physical exercises and stretches, Bible verses, hymns and praise songs. These keep me focused on growing stronger spiritually as I work on physical strength. (More specifics are listed below in the "Bodily/Kinesthetic" section.)

Awareness. Being more aware of my thoughts, more aware of whether or not I feel myself spiritually connected and more aware of God's presence in nature and my surroundings can all contribute to my loving God with all my strength.

Change. A change I have made is to become more engaged in my prayers, either by kneeling as I pray, writing down my prayers, saying prayers out loud, or singing a song that expresses my prayer. These ways have all made my prayer life stronger, and therefore my relationship with God has become stronger and more active, which are ways that I love God with more intensity and with more strength.

Choices. I can choose whether or not I stop and be still, whether or not I kneel to pray, whether or not I write down the things I am grateful for today, etc. I have found that these more engaging routine choices make a difference in the strength or weakness of my spiritual connection.

Throughout. I can focus on having a stronger relationship with God throughout the day—aiming to connect with Him in some way each hour—by trying to remember to say a prayer (perhaps even taking a minute to kneel as I pray), to give gratitude, to recite a verse, or to sing a praise song or hymn.

Total. Since *total* means "completely," "entirely." I can apply this total principle to the entire scope of my daily activities and functioning—to the totality of "what I say or think or do" during each day. To love God with all my strength in a total way means that at least during part of my day I give 100 percent of my mental focus to God. It means aiming to have complete bodily health (as much as is under my control)—eating right and getting exercise and rest. It means having an attitude of complete contentment with where I am and complete trust in God. It means trying to do all my work and have all my interactions with others as if for the Lord.

Using a new ACT acronym for loving God with all my strength

Admitting my weakness, I aim to look to Him for strength depend on Him and trust Him in all things.

Committing to growing/becoming stronger as I would in any strengthening effort, I know that I need to commit and recommit daily to growing in my relationship and love for God.

Training and working at it, I have adopted an attitude of being in training for having a stronger relationship with God, a stronger faith, and a stronger trust. It takes daily work and numerous *reps* or repetitions. It has helped me to view loving God as something that I am in training for.

Multisensory and Multiple Intelligence Activities

Visual

Search for and collect pictures of different symbols of strength. Use these as visual reminders to aim for spiritual growth and strength.

Auditory

Listen to audiobooks, podcasts, recorded sermons, etc. on the topic of spiritual strength.

Visual and auditory

Read books on the topic of spiritual strength. Watch movies on the topic of spiritual strength. Listen to lectures/talks on the topic of spiritual strength.

Kinesthetic

While doing physical exercises and movements, focus on Bible verses about spiritual strength. (See my list of verses relating to spiritual strength.) Choose one specific verse to pair up with a specific exercise or movement and pair up another verse to another movement or exercise. (Make an association between the two.)

Tactile

Copy and write down biblical verses or other meaningful quotes that are meaningful to you and your spiritual growth. Even typing the verses/quotes is a tactile activity.

Multisensory

While performing a movement or exercise, say out loud a verse relating to strength. While performing a movement or exercise, sing a praise song or hymn out loud that is related to strength. Write different verses related to strength in different colors using colored markers to provide visual distinction among the different verses. While writing down a verse or quote, recite it out loud.

Verbal linguistic

Make an acronym about spiritual strength using the word *strong*. For example, I came up with the acronym: *stretching* (my mind, my spiritual connections, to grow stronger), *turn* to God for guidance and strength, *repetitions* (repetitions create strength—how and what can I practice repeating for spiritual growth?), *open* (being open to God's leading and direction will bring strength), *no* to the negative/bad habits and reinforcing instead right habits), *guarding* against things that deter me from strength.

Logical/mathematic

Make a logical flow chart about how to love God with more strength: "If I daily…then…"
Think about how difficult it is to take and receive a gift from someone when your arms and hands are already holding on to some-

thing. What are you holding on to that is preventing you from receiving God's gifts of peace and joy?

Visual/spatial

Use visual imagery as you meditate on common symbols of strength, such as an oak tree, a strong foundation for a building, an eagle, a bear, a horse, an anchor, etc. Picture it in your mind and perhaps sketch it out. Label specific characteristics or qualities related to its strength. Relate those images and characteristics to how you can be stronger in your spiritual life and in your relationship with God.

Create logos and/or draw symbols for strength and growing stronger. Make associations between those and growing stronger in loving God.

Bodily/kinesthetic

Make associations between physical strengthening and stretching exercises and biblical verses and principles about strength.

Recite and/or sing one or all of the following biblical verse while doing repetitions of a strengthening exercise:

- "The joy of the Lord is my strength" (Nehemiah 8:10).
- "In quietness and trust is your strength" (Isaiah 30:15).
- "Be strong in the Lord" (Ephesians 6:10).

Think of *trust* as a muscle. How can bodily exercise principles be applied to making one's trust in God stronger?

Practice clenching your hands while thinking of the worries, anxieties, and ruminating thoughts you are holding on to. Then lift up your arms, opening your hands wide as you say aloud that you are releasing all your cares to God.

Naturalistic

Learn about and think about examples of strength in nature and how those examples can apply to loving God in a stronger way.

Consider things in nature that are very small (e.g., the tenaciousness of a spider's web) as well are those that are very large (boulders, mountains, trees, etc.).

Musical

Do a website search on praise songs and hymns about strength. Then listen to some of them, choosing to memorize one. Some examples are:

- "Strong Enough" by Matthew West
- "You Are My Strength" by Reuben Morgan
- "His Strength Is Perfect" by Jerry Salley and Steven Curtis Chapman
- "Joy of the Lord" by Maverick City Music
- "Be Strong in the Lord" by Church of God Edmonton Youth Choir
- "Quietness and Trust" by Julie True

Interpersonal

Think of what the Bible says about two or three being gathered in God's name and the power of prayer by several people together (Matthew 18:19–20, Psalm 145:18, James 5:14–15, Romans 15:5–6). How can you employ this practice to a greater extent in your life?

Intrapersonal

Reflect on where you currently go or what or whom do you usually turn to for help, advice, strength, etc. Do you try to figure things out on your own? Do you go to a trusted person with whom you are close? Do you go to self-help books? Do you do a search for help on the internet? Do you turn to God's Word and to prayer? Do you use a combination of some or all of the above? Should or could turning to God and His Word play a more valued role as a source of help and strength for you?

Additional Bible Verses Related to Strength

May you be made strong with all the strength that comes from His glorious power... (Colossians 1:11)

I can do everything through Him who gives me strength...(Philippians 4:13)

You will not succeed by your own strength or power, buy by my spirit, says the Lord all-powerful. (Zechariah 4:6)

Finally, be strong in the Lord and I his mighty power. (Ephesians 6:10)

May you be made strong with all the strength that comes from His glorious power, and may you be prepared to endure everything with patience, while joyfully giving thanks to the Father...(Colossians 1:11)

You will not succeed by your own strength or power, but by my spirit, say the Lord all-powerful. (Zechariah 4:6)

Keep alert, stand firm in your faith, be courageous and strong. (1 Corinthians 16:13)

God is faithful, and He will not let you be tested beyond your strength, but with the testing He will provide the way out…(1 Corinthians 10:13)

Now to Him who is able to strengthen you according to my gospel and the preaching of Jesus Christ…(Romans 16:25)

Strengthen me according to thy word… (Psalm 119:28b)

For I long to see you, that I may impart to you some spiritual gift to strengthen you… (Romans 1:11)

I was pushed hard, so that I was falling, but the Lord helped me. The Lord is my strength and my song…(Psalm 118:14)

The Lord is a stronghold for the oppressed, a stronghold in times of trouble. And those who know your name put their trust in you…(Psalm 9:9–10)

Seek the Lord and His strength; seek his presence continually…(Psalm 105:4)

Now to him who is able to strengthen you according to my gospel and the preaching of Jesus Christ…(Romans 16:25)

Strengthen me according to thy word… (Psalm 119:28b)

For I long to see you, that I may impart some spiritual gift to strengthen you…(Romans 1:11)

I was pushed hard, so that I was falling, but the Lord helped me. The Lord is my strength and my song…(Psalm 118:14)

The Lord is a stronghold for the oppressed, a stronghold in times of trouble. And those who know your name put their trust in you…(Psalm 9:9–10)

Seek the Lord and his strength; seek his presence continually…(Psalm 105:4)

In quietness and trust is your strength… (Isaiah 30:15)

Ponderings and Quotes

In the following verse, I noticed that being content precedes receiving God's strength—is this significant?

I have learned in whatever state I am to be content… I can do everything through Him who gives me strength. (Philippians 4:13)

Strength and growth come only through continuous effort and struggle. (Napoleon Hill)

Be sure you put your feet in the right place, then stand firm. (Abraham Lincoln)

Be faithful in small things because it is in them that your strength lies. (Mother Teresa)

With the new day comes new strength and new thoughts. (Eleanor Roosevelt)

(A) calm mind brings inner strength and self-confidence, so that's very important for good health. (Dalai Lama)

Strength does not come from physical capacity. It comes from an indomitable will. (Mahatma Gandhi)

Out of suffering have emerged the strongest souls; the most massive characters are seared with scars. (Khalil Gibran)

Where there is no struggle, there is no strength. (Oprah Winfrey)

Silence is a source of great strength. (Lao Tzu)

Strength is a matter of a made-up mind. (John Beecher)

Some of us think holding on makes us strong; but sometimes it is letting go. (Hermann Hesse)

You have power over your mind—not outside events. Realize this, and you will find strength. (Marcus Aurelius)

CHAPTER 8

Conclusion

As I reflected on the previous chapters, I thought about how the four aspects of loving God—with heart, soul, mind, and strength—are interrelated and interconnected and also how there are some similar themes.

I need to have an awareness or consciousness of loving God with all of these interrelated areas: an awareness of loving Him with my heart, an awareness of loving Him with my soul, and an awareness of loving Him with my mind. I also need to be aware of putting conscious, purposeful energy and strength into those efforts of loving Him. Striving for this purposeful consciousness and awareness is crucial.

It is also important that there be balance between loving God in these ways. Loving God with only my mind—with my intellect and knowledge—without loving Him with true feeling and passion from my heart would not be right. It also would not be right to love Him with only my feeling and passion, without having a biblical knowledge, understanding, and perspective. God is asking that we love him in all these ways without neglecting or putting less emphasis on any one area.

While there are different ways and unique qualities of loving God with all my heart as compared to loving God with all my soul or all my mind or all my strength, focusing on the similarities gave me additional insight. These similarities or recurring themes are the following:

1. *Little by little, step-by-step*—Each of the four aspects of loving God can only be done in small incremental steps. Learning to love God in each of these ways is a process that requires commitment, effort, patience, and an attitude of "progress, not perfection." I know that loving God with all my heart, soul, mind, and strength is not an attainable goal, but I do believe that I need to have a mindset of moving forward in each of these areas. As Van Gogh said, "Great things are done by a series of small things brought together." This is encouraging! By doing small, manageable things, eventually a great thing like loving God more fully can be accomplished. While the thought of loving God with all my heart, soul, mind, and strength can be very daunting, I can focus *right now*, this minute, this hour, on sensing His presence and aiming to love Him through what I do and how I do it in this next hour.

    The concept of starting small with incremental steps is explained by a businesswoman:

    To achieve big goals, start with small habits. It's great to dream big, but the way to achieve big is to start small—through micro habits… By breaking down an ambitious job into smaller, more achievable ones that you build over long periods of time, micro habits help you complete big goals. The idea of making change through small habits isn't new; others have discussed and written about it in the past… But people still struggle to implement them. We're indoctrinated to—and rewarded for—thinking big, not executing small. (*Harvard Business Review*, Sabina Nawaz on hbr.org)

This concept is a necessary skill in successful teaching and is called task analysis. A teacher must know the sequential steps of any objective so that s/he can lead the students in the process of acquiring the skill. Task analysis is especially important in special education, where the steps often need to be broken down into even smaller ones for students with special needs.

2. *Rightness*—I need to be *rightly related* in each of these four areas. Aiming to make my heart *right* means aiming for a *pure heart*; a *right* soul is a soul that is surrendered to Him and one that is Spirit-filled; a *right* mind is purposely and intentionally focused on God; and using my strength *rightly* means devoting my days' purpose and energy to loving Him in all I do by trusting, relying, and depending on Him.

3. *Welcoming, giving consent, and being open to receive*—In all these four areas, I need to have an attitude of openness. I must have an open heart, an open soul, an open mind, and be open to gaining strength in order to love God fully. The act of opening my heart and then surrendering my earthly passions allows me to receive His love. If I let go of my will and allow my soul to be open and uncluttered, I can then be filled with His Spirit. By having an open mind to His priorities, along with mental focus and work on spiritual learning, I can then gain wisdom. It is by first admitting my weakness that I become open to accepting His strength. The act of surrendering and being open allows me to receive God's transformation. This results in the ability to love Him and to love others more fully.

4. *Action required*—In order to love more deeply with each of these areas of myself, I need to make a decision and a commitment to act. What will I *do* to love God more deeply with all my heart, soul, mind, and strength? I need to be disciplined in my spiritual life and daily habits and make loving God more purposeful. As it says in James 1:22

(NIV): "Do not merely listen to the word, and so deceive yourselves. Do what it says." I must make decisions and changes in my daily life that align with loving God more fully.

5. *No action required*—In considering what it means to love God with all my heart, soul, mind, and strength, I learned that I need to *stop* and *do nothing*. I need to respond to and practice the verse, "Be still and know that I am God" (Psalm 46:10 NIV). The most powerful new habit and change for me has been to take more time to be still, meditating on God's presence.

6. *Personal expression*—Using creative ways to express my personal feelings has also been crucial in my spiritual growth. I have used creative expression by

 - writing out my prayers in a *heartfelt* way,
 - privately baring my *soul* to Him,
 - using my *mind* to write a poem or compose lyrics to a song; and
 - using my physical exercise routine as a way to praise and worship Him and to focus on verses about God's *strength*.

Some biblical references indicate that it is desirable in God's sight to express our feelings in such passionate, personal ways with our hearts, minds, and souls.

I poured out my heart, baring my soul to God, my God. (Daniel 9:4 MSG)

Whenever you pray, be sincere…(Matthew 6:5–7 TPT)

I will praise you, Lord my God, with all my heart…(Psalm 86: 6–7, 12a)

My soul is in deep anguish… Turn, Lord, and deliver me. (Psalm 6:3–4)

I desire to do your will, my God; your law is within my heart. (Psalm 40:8)

I will pray with my spirit, but I will pray with my mind also; I will sing praise with my spirit, but I will sing with my mind also. (1 Corinthians 14:15 ESV)

7. *Prayer*—To love God completely with heart, soul, mind, and strength means being fully connected with God, and the primary way we have to connect with God is through prayer. I brainstormed ways that I can be more fully engaged in prayer, thereby hoping to feel more fully connected to Him. I can

- pray out loud and with feeling and passion.
- pray with a prayerful body posture, such as kneeling, bowing down, having hands folded, or with arms outstretched and hands lifted up.
- write a prayer, perhaps using a daily prayer journal. Writing a prayer has often brought about insights and clarity that I didn't see before. This has happened more often when I have written a prayer than when I have silently or verbally prayed. Writing a prayer can be a gift to God, as time and effort are taken to communicate with him.
- aim for balance in my prayers using the different types of prayer: prayers of worship/praise/adoration, prayers of intercession, prayers of petition, prayers of confession/repentance, prayers of thanksgiving.
- sing a prayer.
- illustrate a prayer.
- use movement to express feeling in my prayers.

- compose a prayer that is a poem.
- aim to pray without ceasing, as Paul exhorts us to do in 1 Thessalonians 5:17.
- take time to *really focus* on *praying*.
- be still and *listen* at the end of or during my prayers to allow for a two-way conversation.
- analyze what I am praying for and asking God for, remembering that my requests should align with God's will.
- reflect on *my role* in bringing about the answers to my prayers. Is there something I can do to bring about the desired change?
- continually refocus on God's goodness, greatness, and omnipotence in my prayers, acknowledging that He is in control, that Jesus and the Holy Spirit will advocate and pray with me for those I am lifting up.
- remember to "let go and let God." My trust in God and in the fact that He is in control should be evidenced in my thinking and actions. If later in the day I find myself stressing or worrying about a person or situation that I've already prayed about, I try to remind myself that I have already prayed deeply about that and that they're/it's in God's hands.
- remember the five P's—PLAN when I'm going to pray; PREPARE to pray, get in the right mindset; PONDER my spiritual goals and requests and aim to follow God's leading; PRACTICE balance among the different types of prayer; be PATIENT in prayer sessions, having a relaxed, open-ended period of time when possible as opposed to rushing through prayer.
- *pray* and *praise my way through the day*. I am trying to make a point to reconnect with God every hour of the day. This continues to be a challenge, as I may start out strong in the morning, but by late afternoon and evening, I slack off. It does make a huge difference in

my outlook and attitude when I pray and reconnect frequently.

- *thank God in advance* for anticipated answers to prayers.

O Lord, you hear my voice, I lay my requests before you and wait in expectation. (Psalm 5:3)

O you who answers prayer! (Psalm 65:2)

8. *Throughout the day, every day, at the center of my being—* Our hearts, our souls, our minds, and our strength are each at the center and core of our beings, defining who we are and what we do. I thought about how my heart beats constantly, how my soul can be considered the house of my continual breath, how my mind is at all times active and occupied with some thought, and how some of my muscles, energy, and strength are always working to some degree. Is loving God with all my heart, with all my soul, with all my mind, and with all my strength that much at the center and core of my being? Is loving God a continuous, constant, and instinctive occurrence?

   Some strategies I am using to try make loving God more constant are associating every new hour of the day with time to stop and pray; giving thanks and asking for guidance; listening to Christian radio to fill my mind with praise songs; keeping my mind focused on memorized scripture by mentally reciting a verse, hymn lyrics, the qualities of love, or gifts of the Spirit, etc.; thinking of God the Creator when seeing nature; trying to be aware of and totally content with the unique gifts of each hour of the day.

9. *Dependence/trust/reliance*—In order to love God with all my heart, soul, mind, and strength, I must depend, rely, and trust God in each of these aspects of my myself. I can have a heartfelt desire to trust God, but then in actuality I

continue mentally to try to control a situation. I can *know* in my mind that I need to rely on God for His strength yet rush into a responsibility or activity without first going to Him for guidance and direction.

10. *Worship as a way of life*—I once heard a quote on Christian radio based on a message from Ravi Zacharias that "worship is a way of life." The full quote is, "Worship is a posture of life that takes as its primary purpose the understanding of what it really means to love and revere God" (quotepark.com, Source: *Jesus Among Gods: The Absolute Claims of the Christian Message)*. I think that's the point of the command in this verse—if we love Him with all our hearts, all our souls, all our minds, and all our strength, we will make loving Him and worshiping Him a *way of life* so that we have a constant mindset and awareness of loving God with 100 percent of our being. Our perspective, our main focus and main purpose in life will be to have a close relationship with God. The major point of this book is to incorporate practical, manageable ways to focus on worshiping, praising, and thanking God in everyday routines throughout the day.

Related to this idea of making worship a way of life is a concept my father shared with me about how we can pattern our regular daily lives according to the order of a worship service. I think of that often as I try to start my day with a call to worship, praising God, confessing my weakness, accepting His forgiveness and assurance, affirming my belief and faith, listening to/reading His word and/or a message, offering/giving gifts to Him (the gift of my time), praying for guidance and for others, responding to God with thanks, and going out to serve.

John Maxwell has written about the topic of how we spend our time daily defines who we are. What we do—or don't do—becomes our life's pattern. Along this same idea, Robin Sharma says, "Your days are your life in miniature. As you live your days, so you craft your life. What you do today is actually creating your future. The words you speak, the thoughts you think, the food you eat, and the actions you take are defining your destiny—shaping who you are becoming and what your life will stand for. There's no such thing as an unimportant day" (robinsharma.com).

Kevin Burns, when talking about the Hebrew word for strength and power, which means "muchness," states that "the story of God's extravagant love for the unlovable is His 'muchness' love toward us… When our love toward God is small, enclosed, locked up, cautious, and guarded, it is devoid of the very quality God created within us when He created us in His image. He is muchness and makes muchness out of us…" (kevinburns2019.squarespace.com/home/loving-god-with-your-muchness).

Is there anyone who would *not* want to have a daily close relationship with our perfect, loving Almighty God? A relationship that is characterized by "muchness"—by loving Him more fully with all of our hearts, all of our souls, all of our minds, and all of our strength? We can start *today*

- to form *associations* to connect daily routines with various ways to lift up our thoughts,
- to *change* habits to pray more often and give gratitude more frequently, and
- to stop and sense His presence *throughout* all of the day.

These small, manageable ways will turn into great ways to reshape, redefine, and redirect our lives in an eternally meaningful way.

ABOUT THE AUTHOR

The author has had the lifelong passions of family, helping others, being active in the church, and maintaining a close relationship with God. She is a former special education teacher who has taught in numerous settings and with diverse populations, including public institutions for persons with disabilities, public schools, private homes, and day-care facilities for early intervention, as well as at a university where she taught prospective teachers. She thoroughly enjoyed her past experiences of teaching children and young adults of all ages, from age eighteen months through the graduate college level. She is a wife, mother of four children, and grandmother of seven grandchildren, who are all sources of great joy in her life.